What Readers Are Saying about
Produce, Publish, Publicize

You are helping authors avoid that hell of a scam. It is a big one and a hot one these days. There are so many people trying to get into your pocket and I think you are preventing that over and over again and I salute you for it.
  -Michael Cogdill, Television Anchor, winner of 24 Emmys

Sabrina Sumsion's book Produce, Publish and Publicize is an excellent guide to help independent authors. The book is written in a concise and very informative manner. Any author that takes advantage of the information written in the book will have an easier writing path and will avoid pitfalls that openly wait to entrap the novice. I would highly recommend purchasing this book.
                          -Linda Leon, Former Television Producer

After reading Produce, Publish, Publicize, I would strongly recommend it to anyone wanting to publish their book. Before you spend anything on publishing, spend a few dollars on Sabrina's book. It could save you thousands in the end!
                          -Victorine Leiske, Aspiring Author

Produce, Publish, Publicize

What every writer should know to create an
amazing product, avoid publishing traps and scams
as well as increase sales.

By Sabrina Sumsion

Sanguine Publishing
Dwight, NE

Sanguine Press offers discounts on this book when
ordered in quantity for bulk purchases or special
sales.

Please call 402-484-8124 or email
sabrina@sabrinasumsion.com for more information.

Acknowledgement and Dedication

"…with God all things are possible."
–Matthew 19:26

The Lord gave me the opportunities and ability to learn and understand the complex world of publishing. I would be remiss to ignore his obvious hand in helping me develop *Produce, Publish, Publicize*. This book would also not be possible if several loving people had not supported me and my dreams.

Thank you to my husband for his limitless patience. Thank you to my parents who gave me confidence. Thank you to Lea for introducing me to literary publicity. Thank you to Jack for feeding my huge dreams.

Thank all of you who reviewed my manuscript and helped me refine my message. Especially, thank you Kristopher Miller for your insightful comments and corrections.

Thank you to Victorine Lieske for creating my amazing cover. It is compelling and eye catching. Thank you to my children for the joy they bring me every single day.

Thank you to the fellow dreamers who slave with pen, paper, keyboard and audio software. I cannot even begin to describe the amazing places I have visited, the potent emotions and laughter you have brought me through your amazing books.

This book is dedicated to my wonderful friends and family as well as to you, dear reader. May you learn much about the publishing industry and find success with your passion.

Table of Contents

Section 1: Writing 1

Writing your book 1

Where to Start 3

Original Ideas: 4

Telling a Story vs. Showing a Story 8

Who will type your book? 10

Chapters: Write Three 13

Editors 21

Proof Editors: 22

Content Editors: 22

What to look for in an independent editor 24

Section 2: Publishing 29

Getting a publisher and/or agent 29

Agents 30

Purpose of an agent 31

How to find a reputable agent 33

How to Pick the Right Agent 35

Publishers 43

Types of Publishers 45

E-Publishing 57

Reality Check 63

Avoiding a Publisher's Scam 67

Self Publishing Phenomenon 85

POD vs. POD 90

Section 3: Publicity 93

Publicists.. 97
    What to look for 97
Types of Publicity.................................. 103
Marketing Plan....................................... 103
Writing a Killer Hook 109
Pre-Publication Date Publicity 121
Press materials 123
Review copies.. 125
Face-to-Face Publicity.......................... 126
    Book signings.................................. 127
    Bookmarks and Posters 141
    Print Media...................................... 147
Articles and Print Media....................... 167
Broadcast media.................................... 171
Internet.. 177
Conclusion 185
Book Group Study Guide...................... 187

Preface:
So you want to be an author?

You found your muse. Maybe she woke you at night, caressing your cortex with a novel idea that you think everyone in the world should read. You spent countless hours pounding away on a typewriter, computer or scribbling across napkins and receipts. You read, re-read, revised and perfected your masterpiece. You sit back and sigh. Then you look at the ceiling. You look at the floor. You look at the cat who stares back at you with an expression that says *what are you looking at? I'm just a cat.*

You have your manuscript so what now?

You then hop online and search for hours. You go to the library or bookstore and find books on publishing. You ask everyone you know what steps you should take. Unfortunately, you hear one thing from some people and something completely different from others.

Do you listen to the person who's been rejected by several publishers several times or do you listen to the self published novelist? Do you listen to Aunt Bertha who knows everything about everything? Who do you listen to? What advice do you follow?

Many authors either don't find the answers they are looking for or they find the *wrong* answers. The literary industry is abundant with misinformation and downright lies. Companies misrepresent themselves to make a buck off the back of hard working and desperate authors trying to see a dream come true.

This book evolved because I work as a literary publicist and help authors get attention from media. As I talk to the authors I work with, I find that professionals in the literary industry mislead authors, sometimes unintentionally, but usually uninformed authors are taken advantage of to the tune of thousands of dollars. Sometimes it is an uninformed friend leading the author astray with misinformation read on the Internet but some of the most common problems I encounter are from companies implying promises they never intend to keep.

When you consider that there are approximately 30,000 self published books released each month, you understand that taking advantage of authors is a multi-billion dollar industry! As I have been researching authors who self publish, I have discovered that each author invests an average of $3,000 into publishing each book. If you do the math, that is around 90 million dollars spent each month for publishing services.

Unsuspecting authors' dreams are crushed every day, and many times they don't even know it yet. One author was sure he would sell thousands of copies of his book with my help. I had to explain to him that his cover price and return status would prevent that from being a reality.

In addition, of the authors who spent an average of $3,000 to publish their book, the majority did not make back more than a couple hundred dollars. They added thousands of dollars of debt to credit cards and couldn't even recoup a tenth in sales.

These publishing companies, of course, do not mention on their websites that their authors are struggling to pay off credit card debt and are losing their homes. They only highlight the authors who by luck or intense planning were able to overcome the publishing obstacles the publisher sets up.

This situation inspired me to start a blog dealing with the end ramifications of making the wrong publishing choices. My thought is that when authors can go into the literary world with their eyes wide open, I don't have to break the hard reality of the marketability of their masterpiece to them later.

I realize that authors have a variety of motivations behind publishing their writing. I have broken these authors into three categories: the best-seller hopefuls, the make-a-buck group and the writers for posterity.

The best-seller hopefuls are dedicated to creating a literary masterpiece to which millions of readers flock. These writers typically take writing classes, join writers' groups and guilds and refine their craft as much as their life permits. These authors typically edit, re-edit and edit again diligently before even letting another person review their manuscript. Once they feel good about what they write, they take the time to research the industry and find the publishing houses and agents they want to work with. Then best-seller hopefuls approach the companies on their list after researching the key personnel that cover their book's topic. They wait out the years and years to see their book in print.

Make-a-buck authors typically love writing and have great ideas that pop into their heads. There are two main types of make-a-buck authors; those who have an idea they want the world to hear and those who are developing their product around a lecture series or other income stream.

The authors who are spreading an idea are excited about writing but don't put in the hours, days, weeks, months and years to really flesh out their ideas or their content like a best-seller hopeful. The authors who are basing their product around an alternative stream of income won't turn down sales through traditional channels like bookstores but focus on marketing to those engaged in the other stream of income. For example, a financial adviser might write a book about retirement or investing. He or she is using the book as a resume and uses it to establish him or herself as an expert. The main stream of income is the financial advising and the book is a tool to gain more clientele and consumer confidence.

Writers for posterity are those writers who created a book for their children to read and need a way to bind their creation for their family. These authors are not very interested in sales to strangers. It is not about the money. It is about leaving a legacy so grandchildren and great-grandchildren can know about them after they have passed away.

Produce, Publish, Publicize is for all groups of writers. At the end of each chapter, I speak to the different groups and spell out how important each section is based on each type of authors' goals. Most companies out there will fit one or more group and if you know your goals you will be able to find the correct company that will assist you in reaching those goals.

This book is also divided into three sections that break down the essential parts of selling books. They are writing, publishing and publicity. I have searched out and interviewed the top-professionals in the various fields from publishing to book buying. This book is a culmination of several minds working towards a common goal: helping aspiring authors avoid the scams and traps scattered everywhere in the literary industry.

Section 1: Writing

Writing your book

Being a published author is the dream of an estimated 83% of the adult population in America. It is a long process filled with many, many choices; the first of which is what to write about! Maybe you were born to talk about a particular subject or maybe you have gained expertise over the years in a certain field.

Either way, to have a book, you need to write. That is a daunting task in itself. In our busy lives, who has the time to sit down regularly and type away at the computer for an hour or two each night?

Section 1: Writing

The process of editing is a long and arduous task that takes effort and dedication.

I have been asked for three years to write this book. I can attest that sitting down and typing away for hours at a time can be overwhelming. It is a long process but when done correctly, it is worth every minute of effort.

I encourage everyone who has something to write, to write it. There is technology to assist almost anyone's handicap to enable them to write. There are special keyboards, voice recognition software programs and even devices for people to type without arms! You can view a few options available through Maltron Keyboards on their website www.maltron.com.

The desire to communicate is a universal drive and if there is a will, there is a way.

Where to Start

Obviously, every author must start with an idea. For fiction, you need to have an original idea that has interesting twists and engaging characters. For non-fiction you need information that people want.

If you are writing non-fiction, it helps if you also figure out a way to communicate the information in a unique, enjoyable manner. For example, *Jack's Notebook* by Gregg Fraley (Thomas Nelson, 2007) is a non-fiction book teaching business creativity concepts. Instead of creating a dry, difficult book full of complicated business jargon, author Gregg Fraley used a story line to teach his concepts. Because of his brilliant delivery, his book is used in college and university business courses.

If you are writing non-fiction, take the time to find a compelling way to deliver your concepts.

Section 1: Writing

Original Ideas:

genre

1 : a category of artistic, musical, or literary composition characterized by a particular style, form, or content **2** : kind, sort **3** : painting that depicts scenes or events from everyday life usually realistically[1]

Every story has a general genre. Figure out what your genre is and then start reading. Read the classics in your genre as well as the modern releases. When you have read enough, you can get a feel for what paths have been taken already and sometimes ideas that are over done. The best part of

---

[1] "genre." <u>Merriam-Webster Online Dictionary</u>. 2010.

Merriam-Webster Online. 16 January 2010 <http://www.merriam-webster.com/dictionary/genre>

this "research" is that new ideas can spring into your mind.

A new idea is not the same story with a different name for the lead character but instead a whole new way to handle the crisis part of the story. The basic outline for plotlines has been studied and depending on the researcher, there are 30-48 plotlines in the world.

Think about that. There are millions of books and movies in the world. They all fit into the limited number of basic outlines. What differs is you. What differs is the reflection of life's experiences you bring to the story.

For example: There are many fantasy stories involving magic. Why is Harry Potter successful? There are several new ideas J.K. Rowling brought in to make Harry a household name. The main ideas of finding out you have magic and the struggle between good and evil are old ideas. They aren't enough. Harry found out that he had magic and there was a *present-day* school he could attend.

Most children today secretly wish they would receive a letter of invitation to Hogwarts, delivered via owl, tomorrow. Most adults secretly wish they received one on their 11th birthday. While there are many stories of magic in ancient times or on other planets, this story appealed to the masses because it is a "here and now" twist on old themes. Of course, this was not the only aspect that made Harry Potter a revolutionary idea but the concept illustrates my point. *Find a unique twist and set yourself apart.*

When you have a new idea, tell a few people about it who enjoy the genre. I had an idea pop into my head for a science fiction story but when I started to explain it to my brother who is a big science-fiction fan, he told me that the story line had already been done on a TV show I don't watch. Yes, it was a let down but I'm glad he told me before a heartless editor did. (They're really not heartless but I'll get to that later.)

After you have done your extensive research and found an original idea that your local "experts" have checked off, you need to think about the characters in your story. Until you become best friends with your characters, you really don't know them and can't write about them effectively. Why does the hero wear a watch? Does your villain have a tic?   Why did your damsel in distress become distressed? Maybe you don't need to know the life story of the bartender that serves one drink in Chapter 13 and is never seen again but delve deeply into the inner psyche of the main people you are going to follow around in your story.

Produce, Publish, Publicize

Once you have your characters figured out completely, think about the scenes. Think about what they are going to do in your story and when. Visualize the locations. Is there a signed picture of Marilyn Monroe hanging on the wall of the office of the private eye? How many columns are in the front of the castle your prince resides in? Until you have a clear picture, your readers will not have the visualization needed to immerse in a story.

You're probably thinking, "When am I going to write?" This is the point. You know your characters; you know where your characters are. Now write the first few chapters of your masterpiece.

Section 1: Writing

Telling a Story vs. Showing a Story

A concept I have been teaching a friend of mine is the difference between telling someone what happened and showing them what happened. When you tell someone what happened, it can be as simple as: Jack ran. You have communicated the idea you want your reader to have. Jack moved from one location to another. However, the way you communicate Jack's movement directly impacts the reader's enjoyment and mental picture.

To illustrate my point, compare:

Jack saw his mark and ran to catch him.

To:

Jack crouched in the alley behind a rusty green dumpster. He scrunched his nose and breathed through his mouth to avoid the lingering musk of week old garbage. He scanned the area closely looking for his mark. Jack spotted the man in the black trench coat and red checkered scarf. He surveyed the area around his mark closely looking up, left and right for snipers or anyone tailing his mark. No one else showed any interest in the mark so Jack burst from his hiding place in pursuit of his target. His long, athletic strides quickly closed the gap between the two men.

The essence of both excerpts is the same. They both communicate to the reader that Jack saw his target and both say he ran to catch him. However, the second example shows the reader what is happening and where. It gives the reader a picture to visualize.

Look through your writing and find the places that simply tell the reader what is happening. Replace those sections with a narrative that shows the reader.

Section 1: Writing

Who will type your book?

In our busy society, you may have a brilliant idea for a book or you want to put your knowledge on pages that you can send to others. The problem you encounter is not a lack of will or ideas but instead the lack of time.

When I say a lack of time I don't mean that the commercial breaks during *Desperate Housewives* aren't long enough. I mean that when you get home from the trip to New York you throw your dirty clothes in a pile, crash on the bed for 6 hours then head to the office for a full day of meetings. Then you rush home and change for the fundraiser at which you must make an appearance. You get home, exhausted, at 11PM, check to make sure no vital emails have come in then crash in bed just to be up at 6AM the next day.

Even though writing a book will help you solidify your personal or company brand, you simply do not have the hours necessary to sit down and type out all of your ideas. In your situation, you need to consider having someone else type out your knowledge and organize it into a book.

Produce, Publish, Publicize

You have a couple of options if you need help. You can hire a ghostwriter to create your manuscript under your name or you can find a coauthor. Both options are used by many famous people in the world. For example, any autobiography you read about a president or ruler is written by a ghost writer. Readers understand and accept that these people are too busy to write their own book. Many books with famous names as the author and a mostly unknown person as coauthor are the famous person's ideas typed out and organized by the unknown person.

If you choose a ghost writer you get all of the credit for the information without sharing the author credit. You might even be able to pass it off as your own writing.

The drawback is most people want authentic material directly from the source. For example, if you hire someone to Blog for you, it will typically create negative feelings if the readers find out. The general public craves honesty and many people view hiring someone else to write under your name as dishonest.

If you choose to get a coauthor, you do not have to worry about the general public thinking you paid someone else to make you look good. As coauthors, the public recognizes that you worked together to create the content. It is easier for the audience to accept the information because you are upfront that you had help creating your book.

The drawback to coauthors is your personal brand is mixed with your coauthor's brand. The book isn't completely all about you because someone else's name is on the cover.

In the end, give yourself an honest assessment. Will the public accept that you did not have the time to write a book and a ghost writer was necessary or will the public brand you as lazy? How important is it to your goals behind creating the book that your name be the only one on the cover? Are there benefits to linking your name to another person to enhance your branding? Consider all of these options carefully before jumping into a writing partnership.

Chapters: Write Three

So you have a few chapters completed? Now you have some big decisions ahead of you that will impact how successful your book is. Where do you really want your book to go and who is your audience?

■ Do you want to be a best seller? (Best-Seller Hopeful)
■ Do you want to make a few sales on the side of your regular job? (Make-a-Buck)
■ Do you want to have something to pass along to children and friends but aren't necessarily interested in appealing to the general population? (Posterity Writer)

These are very important questions to ask yourself because this is where you make choices to determine the future of your book.

I want to be very clear on this next statement. You will only be a *New York Times* best seller if a major commercial publishing house chooses to print your book under one their main imprints or you are a marketing genius.

This next statement is very important as well. Major publishing houses' traditional imprints put more precedence on manuscripts submitted by reputable agents and authors that have a proven sales record. They do look at unsolicited manuscripts. One major publisher received 1,000 unsolicited manuscripts in a single month. They corresponded with ONE of those authors. Expect to wait for a year or more before even receiving a rejection letter.

Who are the major traditional commercial publishing houses? Take a walk down the isles of your local major bookstore. Find the best sellers section and read the spines. Typically, you will find the publishing house name there. If you don't see it, open the best selling books and look at the first couple of pages. The publisher's name will be listed there. Now go browse through the genre you write in. The publishing houses you see on those books are the ones you want looking at your manuscript.

Best-Seller Hopeful:
If you want to be a best seller, right now you need to take the 3 chapters you have hammered out

and make the chapters perfect. Edit, edit, edit! Once you are done editing, take it to your friends and have them make suggestions. After you gather all their suggestions, edit some more! Then, find a writing group and have the people in your writing group make suggestions and edit your chapters again. Once you think it's perfect, consider hiring a top-notch line or copy editor to go over your work and make more suggestions. Then, edit your book again. Are you sensing a theme here?

I want you to avoid what I call reader's whiplash. I do book reviews as well as publicity and sometimes I will be reading a good story when all of a sudden, the story line jerks and I get a dazed feeling wondering what I missed. I have to stop, go back and try to figure out the plot line again.

In another book, I'm reading along but feel like I'm reading over speed bumps because there are typos that force my brain to interpret what the author really meant and those typos interrupt the smooth flow of the plot line.

In the end, I want a smooth, enjoyable, relaxing reading experience. Typos, timeline errors, inadequate character development and unexplained plotline jumps leave me feeling like I've been jostled around over dry streambeds for an hour in an old jeep with no shocks.

Section 1: Writing

Remember that readers are your best personal agents. If they enjoy reading your book, they will talk about it to their friends. If they like your book, they will read the next one. If they don't like your book, they will not purchase sequels and they will not tell their friends to buy a copy. Be good to your readers and they will be good to you.

My point is make sure you have the cleanest, most engaging 3 chapters you can possibly manage to write ready. Publishers and agents are readers too and they don't enjoy whiplash. When those 3 chapters are the best they can be, you will start researching publishers and agents.

If you have created a non-fiction book, a solid outline and 3 well written chapters is all you need to have completed before contacting agents and publishers. If you have written a fiction book, the whole book needs to be typed out. The agent or publisher typically will only ask for a sample of your writing first so still refine 3 chapters to submit as a sample.

I have been assured that a writer does not have to have a perfect manuscript to be considered by publishers and agents. So it is not always necessary to hire an independent editor. Not everyone knows what a dangling participle is and a couple of them strewn amongst your otherwise perfect manuscript is not an immediate cause for a rejection letter. BUT if you do not spell "dog" correctly in your manuscript, expect it to end up in the trash bin.

The "traditional" commercial publishing houses have in-house editors to work with you at no cost if they like your idea and if they want to take on your manuscript. However, do not skip editing with friends and family. You wouldn't walk into a job interview without washing your clothes, would you? You need to have a good idea that is well presented to be considered.

Make-a-Buck

Your standards should be the same as authors who want to be best sellers. Your work needs to be a masterpiece to compete with the best selling works that are on the market. If you chose not to wait for a large publisher and you are using a different avenue to publish, always hire a reputable editor.

If your publisher offers to edit your manuscript at a charge, you know that you are not talking to a "traditional" commercial publisher. Since you are not determined to be on the best seller's list, it's okay to consider this publisher as an option. Do your research and find out if the publisher is reputable. A simple Google search with the publisher's name and "scam" should inform you of the publisher's history with authors.

If the publisher has a good reputation, look into their services. I know several writers who hire outside editors on a contract basis. I know of several who do not care about the results and hire anybody to do the work. Do consider several independent editing agencies as well. In the end, it's your money and you get final say on whom you trust. Follow the tips listed on page 27 to find an editor you want to work with.

Since you aren't expecting hundreds of thousands of sales, you can have a lower standard of work. Expect to have your sales drop in proportion to your errors. Reviewers have a hard time giving positive reviews when the storyline jumps or they can't read some of the words. A well-developed, clean story is always better received.

Posterity Writer

Your works do not need to meet the criteria that mainstream books require. Because it is your friends and family that are your target audience, they will be forgiving if you leave out a comma or two. However, do consider that your great-great-great grandchildren's only impressions of you will come from your writing and few other sources. I recommend you leave a good impression.

Before you print anything, send it to friends and family who will catch some of your errors. You may not feel the desire to professionally edit your work but still have others give you input to make the work the best possible.

Section 1: Writing

Editors

For some people, the visual they get when someone says "editor" runs along the lines of the newspaper editor in the Spider-man movies. The visual is a loud, rude man smoking a cigar. While there may be some editors out there who fit that mold, it is not the norm.

Most publishing house editors are very kind but professional. They know what they like to see and they can spot problems easily. Because of understaffing, editors must be brisk when dealing with editorial problems in a manuscript. They may seem heartless when telling you your manuscript needs work but they truly aren't trying to be horrible. They simply don't have the time to walk you through every change that is needed to make the manuscript marketable. They must weed through hundreds if not thousands of manuscripts to find ones that are the closest to ready and which have the best marketing potential.

There are many independent editors in the world as well and if you don't know the two main kinds, you aren't going to understand why you may need more than one qualified person to look at your writing. The two main kinds of editors are proof editors and content editors. One person can fill both positions but most people are naturally good at one or the other, not both. These two can be broken down into more specialized editing tasks as well.

Proof Editors:

A proof editor looks at your writing line by line and checks for typos, incorrect word usage, and congruency with in paragraphs. In my opinion, you should find a competent proof editor first. It's like picking up the trash and miscellaneous items in a room so you can see the furniture.

Content Editors:

A content editor looks at your book as a whole. They are looking for timeline errors, character development, and the overall story. They will help smooth out the story kind of like moving the furniture around in a room to create feng shui.

In my company, there is a top-notch proof editor that knows more about English grammar than

I care to ever learn. She knows how to make a book clean of typos and errors but she is at a loss when confronted with character development.

Another co-worker can revise a whole story progression in her sleep with half her brain tied behind her back. She's not as diligent about typos but the flow of the story improves ten-fold once she has worked with it.

Working together, these two refine a book to near perfection. Separately, they both add to the quality of the book but can't reach the quality level needed for a true masterpiece.

There are really good editors out there who do a good job with both types of editing. The good ones know they are good and charge for the quality of their work. Expect to pay thousands for this level of editor.

There are some editors who are really good but don't know it or believe it so you get a better deal. If you have an editor or company who claims to be a top professional offering to revamp your 300 page manuscript for $99.99, I suggest moving on.

What to look for in an independent editor

The Science Fiction and Fantasy Writers of America (SFWA) created a website www.writerbeware.com to help authors avoid literary scams. These following suggestions are referenced from their webpage: www.sfwa.org/beware/bookdoctors.html.

Request a resume or CV.
You're looking for professional editing experience (preferably with a commercial publisher) and/or professional writing credentials (legitimately-published books, articles, etc.). If the editor has a website, her CV should be posted there (be cautious of editors whose websites say nothing about their credentials). Membership in the Editorial Freelancers Association (US), the Society of Freelance Editors and Proofreaders (UK), the Editors' Association of Canada, or the Council of Australian Societies of Editors are all indications of professionalism.

Ask for titles of some of the books on which the editor has worked.

Commercially published books indicate professional experience and standing, though some good independent editors specialize in self- or POD-published authors (if that's the case, try to get a hold of one or more of the books so you can assess quality). Again, if the editor has a website, the information should be available there.

Be sure the editor's experience is appropriate to your work.

Good editors specialize. Someone whose main experience involves nonfiction may not be the ideal choice to edit your epic fantasy novel.

Verify that the editor really is independent, especially if you've been referred to him/her.

No third party (such as a literary agent) should benefit from your use of the editor's services.

Get references, and check them.

This is important. Other than a recommendation from someone you trust, it's probably your best way to judge an editor's professionalism and effectiveness.

Ask to see a sample of a critique the editor has written.

This will give you an idea of what you'll be getting for your money.

Before making a final commitment, speak or correspond with the editor.

You want to be sure the editor understands your needs, and that you understand what the editor will do for you. You also need to feel comfortable with the editor —not just professionally, but personally —and she with you.

Make sure the business arrangements are clear.

You should know exactly what you'll be paying for, including the scope of the work to be done, the charges you'll incur, the approximate time period involved, and who will be doing the editing (you don't want to choose an editor because of his reputation and discover you've been passed on to a less-qualified underling). Ideally, obtain a contract or a letter of agreement that covers all these areas.

For more helpful hints for writers, please visit the Science Fiction Writer's Association at their website: www.writerbeware.com.

Best-Seller Hopeful:

Expect to work with one or two editors. Find one editor to proof edit first then a content editor after that. Even if you think you can do one or the other just fine, understand that you know more than anyone else about your book. Sometimes, there are vital plot line elements you know in your head but those things aren't spelled out on paper so your readers are clueless. A content editor will help you find the places where you are missing back story.

The large traditional publisher you want to work with should provide top of the line editors at no charge to you. Don't forget to use friends, family and a local writer's group before considering paying for a professional editor. You'll get more value from the editor if you have eliminated the basic typos and plot line errors.

Make-a-Buck:

If you're already not expecting to make a huge amount of money, don't spend a lot of money. Use the family and friends route to make your book the best possible and possibly hire one editor to clean up the final draft. If you'd like the chance to have a better product, you definitely want to hire both types of editors.

Section 1: Writing

If you are using your book as a marketing tool, remember that your book reflects on you as a professional. If your book has typos or isn't clear, you are communicating that you do not pay attention to detail and cannot communicate clearly. If your book is as close to perfect as possible and conveys your expertise, the book will reflect your professionalism.

At least one good editor is *strongly* recommended if your book will be your resume.

Posterity Writers:

Editing is important but you might consider only using friends and family to check your work. Generally, you aren't going to make your editing costs back from book sales if you are mainly interested in selling to friends and family.

Section 2: Publishing

Getting a publisher and/or agent

You're trying to break into the publishing industry as a brand new author and you want to be successful? Maybe you aren't interested in being successful but you still want a book in print. The process of getting a publisher and/or and agent is long and complicated especially if you write fiction. Many times you are stuck between needing an agent to get publishers to look at your work and needing a publisher's offer to get a reputable agent. It's a circular logic that drives many authors to give up or self publish.

There are many excellent books written on getting agents and publishers. They have a lot of detail and they have sample query letters to base your letter upon. Make sure to read several books on these topics to get ideas on the best way to sell your idea! The starting place I recommend is *How to Get a Literary Agent* by Michael Larsen. The book gives honest information on catching the interest of agents.

Agents

Every author who has done any amount of research has heard or read that you need an agent to get published. There are some dissenting voices that declare you don't always need an agent to get an offer from a publisher. Either way, what the heck is an agent and what will an agent do for a book?

Purpose of an agent

There is always the possibility that you are new enough to the literary world that you aren't sure why you need an agent in the first place. The agent is a middleman who takes a cut of your royalties for connecting you with a traditional commercial publisher. If the common adage is "cut out the middle man" why are agents so important?

The top publishing houses you want to be published through generally won't quickly look at an author's idea unless an agent represents them. There are exceptions of course but a top of the line agent will have the contacts to get you out of the "slush pile" and into the "let's look at this closer" pile. The slush pile is where unsolicited manuscripts area placed. This is like back up material for a presentation or a back up singer. People generally look but don't give much attention.

To explain the need for an agent further, what are you more likely to read: an ad that came in the mail or a pamphlet that a friend hands you? The same logic goes for an agent. The agents have the contacts needed to get your manuscript read by a decision maker, know what those decision makers want to read and a give your manuscript a better chance for consideration.

An agent also should have a lot of experience contracting with publishers and getting you the results you want or knows a reputable literary lawyer. It is never a good idea to sign anything without proper representation and a book contract is no different.

There are many rights and provisions that must be negotiated such as foreign rights, film rights, paperback and mass market rights etc. A typical author knows nothing about the varied rights and clauses included in publishing contracts. You can of course hire a literary lawyer without an agent to help you with the contracting part but a literary lawyer typically cannot help you get your manuscript published.

If you decide to search for an agent before a publisher, you must complete your fiction manuscript. Agents typically like a complete project before representing you. It is sometimes different for non-fiction. Non-fiction might find a publisher with only an outline.

How to find a reputable agent

The first and foremost bit of advice I know is never pay an upfront fee for an agent. This could be in the form of a reading fee, submission fee, anticipated expenses or a retainer.

Top agents stand by the manuscripts they represent to the point that they will take a cut on the backend because they are sure they will sell the book to a publisher. The motivations for agents to charge an upfront fee are varied but it's advisable to stay away from them if you are serious about getting results.

The back end percentages you can expect from an agent vary but 15% seems to be the current industry standard. There are some good agents that still charge 10% but they are few and far between. If the agent charges 10%, check their track record. Make sure they are actually making sales.

There are some good agents who will ask for 20%. If they have an excellent record of making large contract sales to top publishers in your genre, they may be worth the 20% to help you publish your manuscript. Just make sure their credits are legitimate.

In the publishing industry, top agents do not need to place ads to gain clients. They get clients through word of mouth. Shy away from agents who post ads if you are determined to be the next Stephen King and you are determined to have the top people behind your efforts.

Another great way to find a reputable agent is to contact those involved with The Association of Authors' Representatives (AAR). They have a website: http://www.aar-online.org/. Not all reputable agents are involved with the AAR. But, you can bet that if they are affiliated with the AAR, they have high standards to uphold and probably aren't scam artists. I would start with the safe bet and contact the AAR agents. An added benefit is if you have a problem with an agent from the AAR, the AAR can help you solve problems and the agent will face repercussions if they were in the wrong.

The Writer's Digest has recognized www.agentquery.com as one of the best website resources for writers five years in a row. It has an online searchable database with over 900 agents from all genres represented. They also have tips for writers and an online networking area to connect with other writers and industry professionals.

How to Pick the Right Agent

When creating your list of agents to contact, remember that agents tend to specialize in a certain genre of books. If you are approaching an agent who represents non-fiction about your new epic novel, you will be rejected. It is better to spend time now finding the right agents rather than incur the cost of printing and mailing your query to a hundred that aren't interested.

Sometimes it is difficult to nail down which genres your books fits into and whether that matches what the agent represents. The genres can be very specific as well. Literary fiction, which focuses on style, is different than commercial fiction which focuses on broad appeal. If a genre is confusing to you, look up the term. Make sure you understand the differences between the various genres to save time, money and prevent unnecessary rejection.

For example, at www.agentquery.com I did a quick search for self-help non-fiction. There were 199 results. On the first web page of results was an agent who represents Literary Fiction, True Crime, Horror, Commercial Fiction, Women's Fiction,

Section 3: Publicity

Humor/Satire, Romance, Young Adult, Thrillers/Suspense, Biography, Memoirs, Narrative and Humor. The results aren't really geared towards my non-fiction topics so she is an agent I would skip.

On the same page of results was another agent who represents Mystery, Commercial Fiction, Women's Fiction, Romance, Thrillers/Suspense, Erotica, History, Politics, Parenting, How-To, Self-Help, Current Affairs, Business, Women's Issues, Finance, Psychology and Cultural/Social Issues. Because she has "How-To" and "Self-Help" listed, I would add her to my list of agents to contact.

Research each and every agent you consider contacting because you want to create a professional relationship with this person. They will be an integral part of your career. You want to *want* to work with them.

A good way to research agents is to find their blog. Agents are aware that Social Media is a powerful tool so many of them post to a blog regularly. Read through many of the agent's posts to get a feel for their personality.

An added bonus to reading their blogs is many have tips on how to pitch them story ideas. For example, Nathan Bransford is a literary agent in San Francisco, CA. On his blog at http://blog.nathanbransford.com/, he has a post giving hints on how to pitch fiction in a query letter. From his post "Query Letter Mad Lib" on March 31, 2008 he gives this tip on creating a query letter:

You know those "mad lib" games you'd play as a kid, where you start off by writing down a list of verbs, places and adjectives, and inevitably the words "snot" and "farted" were involved, which made any story HILARIOUS?

Well, we're going to play query letter mad lib today. Here's how it works.

First I'm going to need these things:

[Agent name], [genre], [personalized tidbit about agent], [title], [word count], [protagonist name], [description of protagonist], [setting], [complicating incident], [verb], [villain], [protagonist's quest], [protagonist's goal], [author's credits (optional)], [your name]

Now, look how your query turns out:

Dear [Agent name],

Section 3: Publicity

I chose to submit to you because of your wonderful taste in [genre], and because you [personalized tidbit about agent].

[protagonist name] is a [description of protagonist] living in [setting]. But when [complicating incident], [protagonist name] must [protagonist's quest] and [verb] [villain] in order to [protagonist's goal].

[title] is a [word count] work of [genre]. I am the author of [author's credits (optional)], and this is my first novel.

Thank you for your time, and I look forward to hearing from you soon.

Best wishes,

[your name]

Nathan's outline is exactly what he wants authors to follow. In fact, he tracks the queries he receives and posts how many people followed his tips on how to pitch him. Unfortunately, not many authors pitch him using his very specific instructions. Your manuscript will rise above the competition if you follow each agent's advice. In other words, agents know what they like and they know what a lot of other agents like. Read what these agents have written, follow their tips and you will have better chances of getting the attention of an agent.

When working with agents *get everything in writing*. There are scammers among agents as well so make sure all the promises an agent makes is on paper.

When you get everything *in writing*, make sure you understand the writing. It is a good idea to pay for a lawyer to read over any contracts you are asked to sign just to make sure there isn't anything you don't understand or you don't see the long term ramifications.

Best-Seller Hopefuls

When the whole manuscript is finished, begin talking to agents. Only contact those who do not charge any sort of fee until after the manuscript is sold and pass the other criteria listed before. If you strike out on a legit agent, then move on to contacting major publishing houses.

Never settle for a questionable agent. You must have implicit trust in this person as they will hold the future of your book in their hands as well as all the money that comes from the sales of your book.

Make-a-Buck

After perfecting your manuscript, you have a big decision to make. If you are writing a cool story that you think a lot of people would like to read, I suggest you start talking to agents then commercial publishers. You have a better chance of making sales this way.

If your product is your resume or supplemental income to a lecture series, you may not want to use a commercial publisher. If you already have a venue for sales set up or you simply want to give/sell copies to clients you already have, you will get a larger cut of profits or a better deal on printing copies by using a different publishing route. In this case, you may not want to contact agents. You can consider self publishing options.

Posterity Author

An agent is not important for your goals. You aren't looking to disseminate thousands upon thousands of books to make a profit. You are interested in your target audience of family and friends and as such, you don't need an agent to represent you.

Section 3: Publicity

Publishers

The actual publishers are the people you really want to work with. They will take your idea and turn it into a marketable product you can hold in your hands. To get a top-notch agent sometimes you need an offer from a publisher first. (Yes, there is circular logic in this industry but I always recommend trying for a good agent before contacting the publishers.) Unfortunately, finding the right publisher can be the hardest and most confusing part of the publishing process.

If you are searching out publishers before agents, you need your three perfected chapters and an amazing outline of your idea ready. Many traditional publishing houses will not accept a full manuscript.

Section 3: Publicity

If your book is fiction, have the rest of your story ready for when the publisher requests your manuscript. If you are writing a non-fiction book, have the outline ready at the very least.

Types of Publishers

There is a broad range of publishers available to authors. The challenge is deciding what your publishing goals are then finding a company that will assist you in reaching those goals.

Because of the varied services and features of companies, sometimes it is difficult to determine what companies are which kind of publisher.

"Traditional" Commercial Publishing House:

I put the word traditional in parenthesis because that word is bandied about widely on the Internet. There are publishing houses that claim to be traditional because they do not charge upfront fees but do not qualify in the real world for the term. The term that actual professionals in the industry use to describe a "traditional" publishing house is a commercial publishing house.

For the purposes of this book and clarification for the average aspiring author, a "traditional" commercial publishing house is one that has high editorial standards; pays a respectable advance for the right to publish your work; pays royalties; does not charge any fees for editing, cover design or other miscellaneous parts of publishing; prints a large run of books; puts a competitive cover price on the book and makes considerable efforts towards publicizing your work.

High editorial standards are the hallmark of large traditional commercial publishing houses. They choose only the best ideas to publish, employ talented editors to help clean up manuscripts until they are perfect and try to make every book as widely accepted as possible for higher sales figures.

A respectable advance may not be six digits or more on a check but will be high enough to compliment an author. If a "traditional" commercial publishing house offers an advance of $1.00, run the other way. They are either insulting your work or aren't truly "traditional" in the sense described above.

Royalties are the reason most authors write. Traditional commercial publishers send royalties on a regular basis, usually twice a year. I know there's math involved in the process and hopefully you have a good agent that is reading through the royalties statements to make sure there aren't any accounting errors.

The "traditional" commercial publisher wants a book to sell thousands if not millions of copies to recoup development, printing and marketing costs. Without a compelling cover, the book will not sell well on the shelves because the adage of people (read customers) judging books by their cover still holds true.

Publishers employ or contract with cover designers to provide provocative covers that will catch the consumer's eye. This is not a cost commercially published authors must bear. The content is as important as the cover so traditional publishers employ their own editors and proofreaders to ensure the content's high standards. Again, traditionally commercial published authors never assume this cost.

When you buy almost anything in bulk, you typically can expect a better deal. This holds true for publishing. Large publishing houses receive a large discount on big runs of books on a per book basis. This enables those publishing houses to put competitive cover prices on their books.

Without a competitive cover price, the books simply aren't going to sell especially when dealing with an unknown author. Traditional publishers are competing for the consumer's dollars so they will mark the book's cover price low to entice the buyer to pick their book.

Publicity is a very important part of any author's success. Publicity is gained through book signings, television, radio, Internet and print media. Best-selling authors show up on network shows and have great book signing successes all across the nation. The publisher usually pays for the travel expenses of the publicity tours and any advertising necessary to promote events.

Lesser known authors have smaller scale publicity tours but still receive attention generated by their publishing company. It is not uncommon for commercially published authors to hire outside publicists to assist the campaign since there are simply too many media outlets nationwide to contact for one person to handle. However, the responsibility to arrange publicity for a book does not fall solely on the author's shoulders with a traditional commercial publisher.

Small Commercial Publishing House:

Small publishing houses are set up the same way as large publishing houses but on a smaller scale. They don't have the revenue to do as much as the large publishing houses do. They have high editorial standards, pay advances, give royalties, assume all the costs of developing a book, print runs of books, set competitive cover prices and work within their smaller budgets to publicize authors.

Subsidy Publishing House:

Subsidy publishing houses are many times an

imprint of a large publishing house but can also be independent companies. The imprint name or subsidy publishing house sometimes has lower editorial standards, it does less to publicize your work, sometimes is printed using a Print-on-Demand (POD) service, it does little to no publicity and requires a down payment before the book is published. They do refund the down payment if sales exceed a certain number. After that, the subsidy publisher sends royalties.

Unfortunately, subsidy publishers tend to mark the cover price of the books higher than competing books to increase the profit margins. This hurts the book's chances of making sales and reduces the chance an author will make enough sales to recoup their deposit. Subsidy publishers may or may not charge for editorial services and cover design.

Self publishing House (Vanity Publishing):
These companies pass all the costs of printing onto the author. The author pays upfront fees for different levels of publishing options.

Typically, the author is required to buy a minimum number of books that the company prints in a run. Self publishing houses are known to use Print-on-Demand as well. The self publishing house does not typically have editorial standards because the author is buying all the books. They are making their money from the author. They are known to offer editing services for a price. The self publishing company does not publicize the books they publish for free beyond possibly sending a postcard or an Email to a list of people the author provides and a flyer to the local media.

The publicity steps are typically ineffective as the author usually tells all of their friends and family about the book before printing. Why would the publisher duplicate the author's efforts? There is little to no follow through on the company's part to ensure each author gets coverage and the author typically does not know which media received a flier to perform the follow up. Sometimes self publishing houses offer the authors the option to buy a publicity package that is also usually ineffective. The exception is when the house offers an actual publicist's services. Then the service is dependant upon the publicist's skills.

This business model typically means you are hiring a printer who also assigns an ISBN number.

Create a Self publishing Company:
You can actually incorporate your own publishing company and publish your own books. You have the most control over your product with

this option. This option does take a lot of work and effort on your part to learn the publishing industry inside and out. You will need to learn about printing standards, distributing, book submission, book publicity and determine a cover price where you can still have some profit at the end of the day. The benefit is you get to take home all the profits from sales.

Printing standards mean that you need to know what weight of paper you want to print on. Twenty pound printer paper doesn't cut it for printing books. You need to know that books have different printing margins so the binders can create clean cuts. You need to know that the quality of printer affects the printed type.

Distribution can be the hardest aspect of the self publishing option. If you want your book to be in bookstores, you need to be listed with either Ingram Book Company or Baker and Taylor in the United States. These are the main companies book stores buy their books from.

To be listed with either one as a publisher you must have a minimum of 10 titles you are submitting. There is a review process and it can take a while to get an answer. Usually, a self published author must use a middle man company to get listed with one of the main distributors but those companies also have a review process.

In addition to being in their system, your book also must be listed as returnable through that distributor. Bookstores won't stock a book they can't send back to the distributor if it doesn't sell.

There is also online distribution. Amazon.com is a major sales outlet that must be considered part of a distribution plans. Barnes and Noble also allows self published books to be added to their online database for customers to purchase from. If you are on one of those sites, other online bookstores will pick up your title as well without any effort on your part.

Because self publishing has gained popularity, there are companies such as Lightning Source and Create Space that have stepped forward to fill part of the distribution need.

Lightning Source is a division of Ingram Book Company. Ingram is one of the two main companies in the United States for book distribution. By using Lightning Source, you get a guarantee that you will be listed properly with Ingram which means that bookstores will be able to order your book. Last time I checked, they do not help you get into online sales venues such as amazon.com or barnesandnoble.com. It is not hard to submit your own book but it is a task of which an author needs to be aware.

My biggest issue with Lightning Source is I know authors who were pressured to set an inflated cover price. Lightning Source has a distribution system most authors want but the price per book charged to authors makes it difficult to keep the cover price down. This is common among all printing companies that allow you to order small volume purchases of your book. Small volume is usually 500 copies or less.

Create Space is a division of Amazon.com. By using Create Space, you are listed automatically on Amazon.com and have that large sales outlet available. However, with Create Space, you have to pay additional fees to be available to bookstores for purchase.

Create Space helps authors get online and offers a better price per book for authors. If you choose the upgrade feature for $40.00, you can purchase a 200 page black and white book for $3.25 each. That's an extra dollar in your pocket for each book sold over choosing Lightning Source.

Lightening Source is the favorite for people who want to be in bookstores. Large chain bookstores such as Barnes and Noble typically will not host an event with an author unless the store can purchase the books through Ingram or Baker and

Taylor. These are the 2 largest book distribution companies in the United States. Lightning Source is a subsidiary of Ingram so titles published through them are automatically listed correctly for bookstores.

I do council new authors to use discretion when working with bookstores. The reason is bookstores demand the option to return, for a full refund, all of the books that do not sell within 1-3 months. A new author is inclined to work to get their book stocked in stores nationwide. I've been hired to do this. It sounds like a great sales strategy but usually it ends up a headache for the author.

If no one knows your name, no one knows about your book. If no one knows about your book, no one will buy the book. If no one buys your book, the hundreds of books you convinced stores nationwide to stock soon come back to you. If you chose Lightning Source to create your book, they will charge you for any money they sent you for books sold *as well as* their cost for printing each book.

One author I worked with received a check for $1,500 from Lightning Source for hundreds of books sold to bookstores nationwide. She did not focus her publicity nationwide so no one knew who she was or why they should order her overpriced books. When all the books came back, she was sent a bill for $4,000 and boxes of books that didn't sell! I encourage authors to only ask stores in areas you are actively marketing to stock your book if you absolutely must be stocked.

Publish-on-Demand:

Publish-on-Demand (POD) companies will print anything that is sent to them rarely turning down authors because of editorial content. These companies may or may not read the manuscript and request editorial changes. Some pay a ridiculously low "advance royalty". These companies may or may not request payment for their services. These companies usually do not provide cover design but some do to make the company look more "traditional". Unfortunately, the covers are rarely compelling. These companies do little to promote your book beyond what you are yourself capable of doing.

True publishing requires planning. True publishing requires that market research is completed before printing. True publishing requires expert cover design and editing. If you can spit out a book in a month, you're not really with a publishing company. You are with a printer. Publish-on-Demand companies are nothing more than glorified printers with a block of ISBNs.

Use great caution with these companies. The only time I would suggest an author use a Publish-on-Demand company is if they choose all options that cost nothing and they only are selling to family and friends. (Writer for Posterity)

E-Publishing

Because ePublishing is a new and still non-standardized category, I decided it needed a section all of its own. ePublishing encompasses selling your book in pdf form online as well as selling a specially formatted version of a book online sent to an electronic device the customer reads.

Ebooks have been around for a few decades as of this writing. In 1971 Michael S. Hart started Project Gutenberg. Project Gutenberg's goal is to spread eBooks. There are over 30,000 titles in Project Gutenberg's database which holds public domain books.

The very first text scanned into a Xerox Sigma V mainframe computer at the University of Illinois was the Declaration of Independence. This particular computer used happened to be one of the 15 original nodes that became the backbone for the internet.

In 1993, Zahur Klamath Zapata created the first software to read a book. *On Murder Considered as one of the Fine Arts* by Thomas de Quincey was released using Digital Book v.1. That year, Digital Book, Inc released 50 titles on floppy disk.

Section 3: Publicity

In 1998 Kim Blagg purchased the first ISBN assigned to an eBook. Her company Books on Screen launched several electronic books but the buying community wasn't really interested. The first eBook readers were released around the same time but again, the buying public wasn't very impressed.

Since the popularity of Adobe's PDF program, many authors and publishers have ventured into releasing books by PDF. Releasing a book in electronic format generates less production costs, can be made into a turn-key business as well as makes it easier to release more books.

An electronic book does not have to be printed out on paper, costs nothing to ship and does not wear out. Several publishers use the eBook format in an effort to be more "green". Trees are not used to create an eBook. There are no large printing machines that use resources to run required when releasing an eBook.

If the author can find his or her niche audience, it is very easy to set up a turn-key revenue stream for his or her book. Customers can buy the book, pay online and have the book delivered to their inbox immediately. The author does not need to do anything during the sale. There is no inventory to ship and the payments are processed automatically by a company like PayPal.

Releasing an eBook can be easier as well. Ordering proofs from the printer is not necessary, distribution is a simple task and making the book into sell-ready condition is as easy as converting it to a PDF. A physical book requires juggling more details.

There are many positives to releasing a title as an eBook but there are drawbacks as well. The drawbacks to releasing a book in PDF form have been controlling where the book goes after the book is downloaded, a small market and difficulty getting coverage for the release.

It is easy to forward an email to a thousand people with a PDF attached. Even if you password protect your PDF, the customer can give others the password. Many readers do not respect a copyright and see nothing wrong with forwarding good information. It is the same problem the music and movie worlds are dealing with.

Because there was no way to control the dissemination of information after the sale, commercial publishers have not embraced this method of e-publishing. Some people might wonder if this is a valid reason to ignore ePublishing because you can read a book and hand it to someone else. Publishers have no control over dissemination after the book is sold to a customer.

The true issue lies within the replication. Your paper bound book will not sprout babies that you can pass out to several people at the same time. You can loan it to only one person at a time. With PDF books, they can be replicated digitally - quickly. If people were so inclined, an amazing book could be purchased once then sent to every person in the world with an email address. This is not a good sales model for the creator or publisher.

eBooks take dedicated readers. Most readers do not enjoy reading a book off of a computer screen. It is a nuisance for speed readers who are constantly scrolling. There are also readers who simply love the feel and smell of a printed book. Because of these factors, it is difficult to create a large online customer base for PDF books.

Mainstream media does not recognize eBooks as a product. Mainstream media wants a physical product that you purchase from a sales outlet to promote. Also, without the validation of commercial publishers, it is widely felt that an eBook isn't a "real" book.

Overcoming those limitations have kept eBooks in the background until the release of the Kindle and Sony Reader. The Kindle and Sony

Reader and now the Apple iPad have overcome some of the drawbacks preventing commercial publishers from widely embracing eBooks.

Kindle eBooks are downloaded to a single device linked to a customer's account after purchase. A customer cannot forward their copy to friends. The only way they can let another person read the book is to physically hand the other person the electronic device. This model puts the distribution of post-sale copies back to the paper-bound distribution which makes publishers happy.

The current debate as of this book's publication is about the pricing of eBooks. Publishers are desperate to see a profit off of their books and fear that low priced eBooks will prevent that bottom line from being met. Right now, there are disputes between large publishers and sales outlets such as Amazon.com regarding the sales model and the price. In the end, the consumers will speak with their money. If no one buys the eBooks, the prices will drop. If sales are steady, the price will hold or rise with inflation.

Section 3: Publicity

Reality Check

In the minds of the big players in the industry, everything that isn't a large or small traditional commercial publishing house is a vanity press. If you are trying to set up a book signing with your local Barnes and Noble, they don't care if you paid for the printing costs or not. If you aren't published with a major imprint, you are self published through a vanity press to them.

In fact, Barnes and Noble has a standing policy discouraging locations from stocking any book that is published through a vanity publisher. The harsh reality is that not enough people know about the book. Typically, the cover price is too high to be competitive. Your area locations may make an exception for a local author but they do not hesitate to return any books that do not sell in a short time period.

This may be hard to swallow if you have already printed through a vanity press. The long and the short of the issue is you don't have a publisher's marketing dollars behind your work. Without the money and publicity, you aren't going to hit the best seller's list.

Many people think this is an opinion only held by the elitists in the publishing industry. If you have your own sales channels lined up, this might not even affect you. If you are relying on bookstore sales to launch you into a better life, do not publish with a vanity press.

Best-Seller Hopeful

If you want to be a best seller, your publisher will have a lot of say in whether that dream will be a reality or not. You should have read about agents already and I strongly encourage everyone that wants to top the best seller list to refuse to publish with any company that does not have an established list of best selling authors or does not exclusively go through an agent. There are rare success stories of authors being picked up by traditional publishers after printing with a vanity press but always try to interest a traditional publisher first.

Make-a-Buck

Your publisher affects the marketability of your book that in turn affects how many sales you will make. You should always try for a top publisher first and then look at smaller publishing houses.

If these two routes are closed to you, you need

to decide if you are more concerned about publishing control than cost. If you want control and have the money to spare, creating your own publishing company may be appealing to you. If you don't have enough time to devote to a company, having a self publishing company handle the book is the next best thing as you pay for the publishing options.

If you don't have extra money to burn and you are determined to publish, then look at the Publish-on-Demand avenues. Because you have already tried the optimal free publishing avenue (traditional commercial publishing), this is your only option left. You will encounter stigma because of the publisher name on the spine of your book, typically have a high cover price that reduces sales, may or may not be returnable and you are on your own for effective publicity.

Posterity Writers

Since you are writing for a select group of people, you goal should be to create a work that is clean with as little cost as possible. Choose a publisher who does not charge authors for anything. Do not opt for any of the additional services like editing or in-house publicity campaigns. The services Publish-on-Demand companies provide tend to be mediocre at best. You will be better off hiring independent contractors for those services if you really want them.

Avoiding a Publisher's Scam

I mentioned before that this industry is fraught with scams. There are publishing houses that claim to be traditional but aren't. There are companies that have hidden fees or make promises off paper that they never intend to follow through on. I have compiled a list of questions to ask publishers and the answers you want to receive.

Is my book returnable to the distributor?

Big bookstores like Barnes and Noble, B Dalton, Walden Books and Borders order through distributors, not the publisher. The main distributors in the United States are Baker and Taylor and Ingram. For bookstores to consider stocking your book, they must be able to order through the distributor *and* return through the distributor.

If the bookstore can't sell your book to the public, they want the option of packaging up the books and sending all the ones that didn't sell back to one location. There are thousands of book publishers and the stores don't have the time or desire to pack a box for each publisher.

Section 3: Publicity

Book publishers sometimes claim their books are returnable but they mean that the store can send it back to them and not the distributor. Bookstores don't like that. Bookstores deal with hundreds of different publishers and creating a box for each one to return books wastes employee hours. You will not get many, if any, signings and you will not get books on the shelf if your book is not returnable to the distributor. Get it *in writing* that your book will be returnable to the distributor by a certain date and that the distributor's information will be correct.

You must *have this in writing as some publishers will drag their feet to follow through on this issue.* They can say your book is returnable until they are blue in the face but if Ingram's iPage says your book is non-returnable, that is what the bookstores believe. If you have a guarantee that the distribution will be correct in a timely manner *in writing*, you have legal ammunition against the company if you incur losses because of their negligence.

For example, you hire an outside publicist to set up book signings and promote those events for you. You pay the publicist thousands of dollars and they make call after call but no one will host you because your book is listed incorrectly. You have lost thousands because the publisher was negligent in getting your profile listed correctly.

I know this happens first hand because I have been the publicist looking at a copy of the author's receipt for return status (yes, some companies charge you money to be returnable) yet I'm on the telephone with a bookstore and they are telling me the book is not returnable according to the distributor.

Unfortunately, I have never had an author get a deadline *in writing* and therefore entire publicity campaigns have been ruined by negligent publishers. Again, *get it in writing* that the publisher is responsible for and accountable for listing your title correctly with the distributor.

Are you printing a run on my books or are they Print-on-Demand?

As I wrote before, a run of books is when a large quantity of the same title are printed at one time then stored in warehouses. Print-on-Demand books are stored electronically then printed as there is demand.

Why does this matter? In the end, the printing method affects your cover price and marketability. A run of books is less expensive to print per book so the publisher can set a lower cover price to be competitive and still make a profit. However, there is an upfront cost to do it this way and there are warehousing costs. The publisher must be confident that there is a large demand for the book to take this risk.

Also, Print-on-Demand carries a stigma that bookstores aren't crazy about. They will be more interested in hosting events and stocking your title if your books are printed in a run.

There are many people who call Print-on-Demand the wave of the future. There are book vending machines being created where you push a button and a book is printed, bound and popped out.

Right now, the costs are simply too high to compete with brick and mortar stores and printing books in a run. Maybe in the future POD will become a more cost effective way to create books but at the moment, commercial publishers and printing a run of books are the way to go.

What will my cover price be?

Get the cover price *in writing* before you sign anything. Now go to your local bookstore and find books in your genre that is the same binding (hardcover or paperback) and have the same number of pages. What are those cover prices? If there's a difference of 10-20%, you're still in a competitive range. If your book is double or triple the price of similar books in the bookstore, your publisher thinks you aren't going to sell many books and they are jacking up the cover price to increase their profits.

If you want to be a best seller, run away from jacked up prices. If you just want to sell to family and friends, this is OK if your friends and family are comfortable financially. For a high cover price, make sure you're not paying any upfront fees such as cover design, electronic set up or distribution charges like a subsidy publisher asks.

Are you going to charge me for editing?

A traditional publisher will either turn you down because of your editing or they will cover the expense to clean up your manuscript themselves. Publishers that offer in-house editing services for a fee offer it to make more money.

Think of it as a conflict of interest. A publisher who is offering editing and other miscellaneous services at a charge will be less inclined to focus on selling your book and more inclined to sell you side services. You want to work with a company that is motivated to help you sell copies of your book. If they receive payments from you that help keep them in business, they do not need to focus on selling your book.

The other issue I have is that these companies don't always hire top of the line editors. If I had a dollar for the number of times I tell an author about typos and he or she responds that they paid for editing through their publisher, I would be a wealthy person on my own island snorkeling every day! If you have to pay for editing, find an independent professional worth the fee.

How will you publicize my book?

A traditional publisher will put a lot of time and money into publicity. The amount will depend on the size of the publisher of course but they have a vested interest in high book sales. For there to be high book sales, the general public needs to be aware of a book and feel the need to read it.

The first thing I suggest is getting *in writing* whether through Email or directly in your contract the detailed steps the publisher takes for publicity. This is called a marketing plan. Get it *in writing* as this is insurance for the future if you find out they aren't doing what they said they would do.

If the publisher asks for a list of your friends and family to notify about your book, then expect little else publicity-wise from them. This is the first sign you will be doing a lot of your own legwork and you should consider an outside publicist. Honestly, you have probably already told everyone you are publishing a book. Why do you need the publisher to duplicate your efforts?

If they tell you they are contacting your media, make them be specific *in writing* exactly what their efforts will be and how many hours they will spend on your book.

A particular Publish-on-Demand company declares they are a "traditional" publisher but the only media contacts they perform is sending a flyer to your local media notifying them of the book. There is no follow up. There are no targeted media groups contacted nationwide. Most authors find themselves told months after publication they should consider hiring an outside publicist if they want to see more sales. By that time, it can be too late for a truly successful publicity campaign.

Ask for the marketing plan the publisher developed for your book. A commercial "traditional" publisher will at least have a general outline of marketing efforts created before they officially take on your book.

Large traditional publishing houses are promoting your book months before a single official book is printed. They send out advance review copies or galleys to the top reviewers like *The New York Times* and other venues targeted to your book's topic. If your publisher isn't sending out free galleys for publicity months in advance of your release date at their own cost, they aren't a truly traditional commercial publisher.

What are the distribution responsibilities of the publisher? What are my responsibilities?

I represented an author who published through a supposed traditional publishing house. It would stand to reason that the publisher, who should have a lot of experience with distribution, would guarantee that the book was listed correctly with all major sales venues before the release date. This includes Amazon.com, BN.com, Barnes and Noble stores and both distributors Ingram and Baker and Taylor.

The book wasn't listed on Amazon on his release date. It was not correctly listed for a week after his book was released. The book wasn't listed with the distributor Ingram at all and Baker and Taylor had incomplete records until I started giving the author ammunition to get the publisher to do something about it.

Four months into his publicity campaign you still couldn't go to Barnes and Noble and order the book much less find it on the shelf. Since Barnes and Noble can't order it, the locations wouldn't host an event with the author. His whole campaign was crippled because the publisher did not do things correctly. Unfortunately, there was no clause in the contract stipulating the publisher's responsibilities.

The publisher needs to have distribution set up

and ready before a single book is printed. Make sure you have a stipulation in the contract detailing what the publisher is going to do for your distribution. Ask questions to find out what that leaves for you to do.

What if I am unhappy with your services? Are you going to sue me if I complain on a public forum?

I have been hearing rumors that some contracts stipulate you cannot complain about the company on any public forum. This includes Internet forums or blogs. Unfortunately, you don't read about this sort of thing because the writer is liable to be sued if he or she makes "defamatory remarks." Watch closely for anything in the contract impeding your First Amendment right to state your opinion about your experience with a publisher. (Of course don't take that as the right to spread lies.)

The only exception I am inclined to make is if it is a traditional publishing company with best-selling authors on its published list and you are being published through their main imprint for a huge advance. Then you are dealing with a professional company and expect to go through professional routes to clear up any grievances.

Another facet to this scam is a company trying

to intimidate authors who complain about their services. I worked for an author who published with a certain notorious company that scams authors. She didn't read the fine print or research the company so the realization that she wasn't going to sell millions of books was hard for her. She complained to the company about their business practices and she got an Email demanding an apology for her opinions! I'm proud to report that she didn't apologize for stating her mind. Intimidation to keep authors in their place is not a flattering tactic for a publisher to use.

Make sure you don't sign anything with any language implying you can be sued for stating your opinion on their services and if the contract has a clause like that, consider a different publisher.

What will the quality of my finished product be?

This is a very important question but a hard one to get a straight answer that you will understand. One author sent me his book that was subsidy published and the margins were horrible. You couldn't read the book without breaking the spine. The reality is margins matter.

I just received a telephone call from another author who published through a vanity press before she realized what she was doing. She recently ordered 25 books for a book party. When she received her order, she flipped through one of the books. To her horror, the margins were different all through the book. On some pages, the writing went almost off the page. On other pages, you had to break the book's spine to read the words.

This happens to vanity and Print-on-Demand customers more than these companies would like to admit.

I worked with another author that thought he had a traditional publisher but it was actually a subsidy imprint of a larger label. I read through his final book and the printing quality was horrible to the point that letters were missing from the middle of words. If half of your letters are illegible, it will frustrate readers and you risk losing fans. The print quality matters.

If you choose to pay for an in-house cover designer, you may not be getting a professional graphic artist. Some companies give you a selection of template covers to choose from. Others assign a cover designer. In the end, once you decide on a cover, get outside opinions from people that will give you honest answers.

I worked with an author who hired the in-house designer to create a cover and he was thrilled with the end product. Unfortunately, it was a juvenile cover that turned people off immediately. Book reviewers stated in their reviews they wished he had a different cover. If your cover doesn't excite people, tell the cover designer to redesign.

If you want sales, make sure you get honest opinions about your cover and even if you like it, it's the general public's opinion that matters when it comes to sales. People still judge a book by its cover. The cover design matters.

How long until I see my book in print?

This is a big tell about the size and status of the publisher. A traditional publisher will tell you expect a year or more unless your book is in answer to a topic that is current in the news. They have an editorial schedule to follow and your book will be put at the end of the line behind established authors.

The exceptions are for manuscripts that deal with the legacy of someone famous that just died such as Michael Jackson or a topic such as insider trading when a celebrity like Martha Stewart is accused of the crime. A seasonal book can be delayed until the next year; a fiction book can be released at any time. You will only get bumped to the front of the line if you deal with a topic that is all over the news and the publicists can get you tons of media time if the book is released immediately.

The publisher needs to give their in-house editors and support staff time to go over your work with a fine-tooth comb and eliminate any typos and inconsistencies. Part of the year lead-time could be spent with you, the author, rewriting a chapter or two that aren't smooth. Authors need to have patience when dealing with top publishers. They will work very hard to make your book the very best is can possibly be. They know what they are doing so let them have time to do their jobs.

If you are told you could see your book in print in a week or as soon as a couple of months you have probably found an "author mill". The companies who will spit out a book that fast don't care about the quality of each book but rather the quantity of books they can publish each month. This is a poor sign for best-seller hopefuls and sometimes make-a-buck authors. If you are a posterity writer, this may be acceptable depending on the answers to the other questions.

Best-Seller Hopeful
Ask all of the above questions!

Make-a-Buck
Ask all of the above questions!

Posterity Writer
Ask all of the above questions!

It's always prudent to get all of the details before making a decision about which company to work with. Once you know exactly what the publisher is going to do for you and what you are responsible for, you can make an informed decision about whether the company can help you achieve your goals.

Section 3: Publicity

Self Publishing Phenomenon

With a simple Google search, it is possible to find hundreds if not thousands of websites dedicated to self publishing. I have been wading through this mess myself as I have been pondering which route is best for me and my goals. From the printing companies that will print any number of books for you, to the self publishing companies that charge you thousands of dollars to publish your book, to Publish-on-Demand companies, writers are given many options to pick from when self publishing.

Bowkers released an announcement of publishing numbers for 2008 in May of 2009.

Bowker Reports U.S. Book Production Declines 3% in 2008, but "On Demand" Publishing More than Doubles
New Providence, NJ - May 19, 2009 - *Bowker, the global leader in bibliographic information management solutions, today released statistics on U.S. book publishing*

*for 2008, compiled from its Books In Print®
database. Based on preliminary figures
from U.S. publishers, Bowker is projecting
that U.S. title output in 2008 decreased by
3.2%, with 275,232 new titles and editions,
down from the 284,370 that were published
in 2007.*

*Despite this decline in traditional book
publishing, there was another extraordinary
year of growth in the reported number of
"On Demand" and short-run books
produced in 2008. Bowker projects that
285,394 On Demand books were produced
last year, a staggering 132% increase over
last year's final total of 123,276 titles. This
is the second consecutive year of triple-digit
growth in the On Demand segment, which in
2008 was 462% above levels seen as
recently as 2006.[2]*

---

[2] Bowker, Bowker Reports U.S. Book Production
Declines 3% in 2008, but "On Demand" Publishing
More than Doubles,
http://www.bowker.com/index.php/press-
releases/563-bowker-reports-us-book-production-
declines-3-in-2008-but-qon-demandq-publishing-
more-than-doubles (May 19, 2009)

Aren't these numbers amazing? We have access to so many view points and so many imaginations! On the other side of the coin, how many of these authors self published with a clear marketing plan, sales channel and platform to really take off?

The motivations to self publish have changed over the years. Many times a book is written as a sales tool for a company or person. In this case, it is not necessary to try to find a traditional commercial publisher. It's probably not a good idea to pursue traditional publishing at all as they might demand a cut of all profits garnered from customers or clients found through the book. (Never forget that publishers are a business looking for every revenue stream possible!)

Another reason to avoid spending time on a traditional publisher is when you cater to a smaller niche audience of which traditional publishers typically aren't interested.

If you are older and don't feel you have enough time left to wait years to see your book in print like traditional publishers demand you may be motivated to go with a self publishing option.

Still other authors venture into self publishing because they are scammed by companies calling themselves "traditional" publishing houses and sell their rights for a one dollar advance.

Any way an author enters the self publishing arena, they become a member of the majority of published authors in America. The numbers of these authors have swelled to a point where the self published stigma is slowly losing strength.

An unfortunate reality for self published authors is they will typically spend more money than they will make. Even with professionals from a traditional publisher in an author's corner, many books fall flat and money is lost. The benefit to a commercially published author is the publisher incurs the costs. A self published author must bear the loss on his or her own.

Self publishing doesn't take purchasing thousands of books anymore. It doesn't have nearly the negative stigma it used to carry. It isn't the kiss of death for the success for your book, but it is vitally important to look at the numbers and make sure it is a sound investment!

Do you have a solid marketing plan? Printing a book and casting it out to sea and hoping people will flock to it usually fails. You need to develop a platform and create a following. You want to develop personal ambassadors.

As an example, my mother is a personal ambassador for Stephenie Meyer. She has read all four 550+ page books 10 times. That isn't an estimate either. She just told me she's done with the tenth reading of book four. Every person my mother meets will end up hearing about the Twilight series and how every person on the planet should read the books. Due to the popularity of the books and the fact that there are now almost three movies out based on her series attests to the fact that Stephenie has a lot of personal ambassadors.

Professional marketers, like the ones you would work with if you are published with a commercial publisher, work very hard with each author to develop a platform that will attract people and cause them to bring more people to the platform.

For congruency in this book, section 3, Getting the Word Out covers marketing plans.

POD vs. POD

Much confusion in the self publishing arena stems from confusion about the acronym POD. The problem is it can mean 2 things that are hard to differentiate. POD either means Print-on-Demand or Publish-on-Demand.

Print-on-Demand is a printing method. Your publisher can have your books stored electronically and printed when there is a demand for it or the publisher can print a run of books and store the physical copies in a warehouse.

Publish-on-Demand is a publishing house's business model. Publish-on-Demand means that the publisher publishes exactly what is sent to them shortly after it is sent to them. Some people assert that there is no such thing as Publish-on-Demand. They assert that the publishing process takes too much time to be on demand. There are still companies out there that pretend to be publishers when they are little more than printers. Because they exist, I still want to make sure people understand POD *can* mean two different, yet similar things.

Why do you care? Print-on-Demand isn't necessarily the spawn of the devil. It is useful for classic books of which there is a small but constant demand. Being associated with a publisher that churns out any old manuscript sent to them means Publish-on-Demand. That is never a positive thing.

To tell the difference, remember that a quick turn around time doesn't mean your manuscript is perfect. It's usually a sign that the publisher doesn't care about the quality of the product. If the publisher tries selling you editing services or sells a manuscript evaluation service, they are probably a Publish-on-Demand company.

Depending on your goals as a writer, a Publish-on-Demand company might be what you are looking for. There are Publish-on-Demand companies such as Publish America that do not charge upfront fees to see your book in print. They do, however, encourage you to purchase many books at inflated prices to recoup costs.

If you are a writer for posterity, you might want to choose a company with this business model so you can avoid set up fees like some companies charge, order several copies at your "discounted" author rate and sell or give the books to your friends and family.

Section 3: Publicity

For Print-on-Demand, just because the publisher uses this printing model does not necessarily mean they are a bad company to work with. Do your research and find out what books they have released, what the company is planning for marketing and if there are hidden fees. If the publisher uses a Print-on-Demand model, you can typically expect either a higher cover price or a smaller cut of royalties.

Depending on your goals and what other services the company offers, a Print-on-Demand publisher might work for you.

I will emphatically state that a best-seller hopeful should avoid either type of POD company.

Section 3: Publicity

Publicity is to books as wings are to birds. A bird can't take off and soar without wings and a book will not be successful with out publicity. The whole point of publicity is to make people aware of your book and encourage them to buy it. It stands to reason if no one is told about your book no one will buy it. This logic is what makes the choice about publishers imperative. If your publisher isn't telling anyone about your book then the responsibility falls to you if you want sales.

Best selling authors are a vital part of their own

publicity campaigns. They put in countless hours and large amounts of effort telling people about their book. They spend hours at book signings, radio interviews, television interviews, Internet interviews and do everything possible to generate consumer loyalty. They make fools of themselves and performing stunts in the effort to get more attention.

Best selling authors do not sit back and expect sales to come pouring in. The successful authors work very hard to *make* their book a success. All the amazing stories you read and hear about a vanity author being picked up by a major publisher are because the author spent countless hours telling the public about themselves.

In fact, publishers are starting to believe that the author *must* put in just as much work as the publisher for each book. No longer can a best selling author send the book off to a large commercial publisher and expect to pick up royalty checks in the mail. The author goes on book tours, is scheduled on countless radio and television shows and generally works harder on promotion than they did on writing.

Expect to be the biggest part of making your book a success. No matter how much people talk about your wonderful book and what they will do for you, they do not love the book as much as you do. Take your passion and share it!

The publicity steps I outline can be done with or without a publicist. As a publicist, of course I recommend you hire one. A publicist gives credibility to your book, they can access media contact information quickly and have avenues to contact those media effectively. A good publicist will also have established relationships with media outlets to help garner more publicity.

A big benefit to hiring a publicity company is the media contact lists. You can set up an agreement to purchase media contact names targeted for your book. If you are very driven and want to do everything yourself, you can subscribe to a database of media contacts but expect to pay around $3,500 each year. When you consider all the hours invested and costs involved, it is usually a better deal to hire a publicity company or purchase the specific contact names from them.

In my mind, the next biggest benefit of hiring a publicist is they take all the rejection for you. Out of a list of 200 targeted contacts, I expect maybe 5 interested media contacts in a good week. It can be very discouraging to hear no 195 times every week. The publicist runs interference for you so you do not have to receive all of the rejection.

Section 3: Publicity

Publicists

If you search for publicists on the web you will find many companies that provide publicity. From the one-man operation to a huge company paying hundreds of employees, you want to find a good company that will work hard to promote your book.

What to look for

In a publicity company, you want a decent price, a reputable company and results. Anything less would be ineffective and detrimental to your budget.

A decent price is the hardest thing to find with publicists. There are some publicity companies that charge five digits for their services. These companies typically will only work with traditional publishers and the author does not pay their fee. There are some publicity companies that charge $5,000 or more a month. There are some that charge only $1,000 a month. There is a rather big spread between what companies charge and typically it boils down to overhead.

If you are looking at a business in a New York penthouse suite, the authors are paying for that suite. Does a penthouse suite make a publicist better at publicity? No. It means they have expensive taste and the authors will bear the cost. Might they have the contacts to take your book to the best seller list? Maybe. Look deeper and make sure you are getting your money's worth.

Is a $1,000 a month publicist bottom basement when it comes to results? Maybe but if they are in an area with a lower cost of living and that publicist only represents 5 authors a month, that is still $5,000 dollars a month in that company's pockets. The publicist usually sees $2,500 of that.

When looking at the cost, balance the reputation of the company. Ask for references and contact those references. In my opinion, a simple Web search will expose more about a company than references. One or two complaints and the company should be okay as long as there are satisfied, verifiable authors as well.

Look for honest complaints that come from verifiable past authors of the company. Unfortunately, there are smear campaigns in the publicity world. If the person who posted on the Internet doesn't identify themselves or at least plug their own book, you can bet it's a competing company trying to drive business away for whatever reason.

However, if you can't find anything nasty or nice from a verifiable source, the company is probably new. In that case, see if the company is an offshoot or if it is someone who just decided one day they would be a good publicist. Many times new companies that are offshoots of other companies cannot advertise the work they did for past authors because it conflicts with the former employer's ownership of all good will derived from contracts. In this situation, you have to decide if you are willing to take a chance or not.

The typical publicity company's results can be judged by contacting past clients and finding out how successful the authors feel the publicist was. Did the publicity meet all of the goals of the campaign? Were they flexible enough to work with the author to make the best campaign possible? Try to find out as much as possible about book signings, print media and broadcast media secured for each author.

Should a publicity company guarantee or imply book sales from hiring them?

No. No publicity company can guarantee their efforts will turn into sales. Can they guarantee they can increase your *odds* of making sales? Yes. The more people that know about your book, the better chance someone will buy it.

Some publicity companies have you pay per interview/article they secure for you. Some publicists are just that good and have that many connections in the broadcast world that they make a good living being paid per interview.

For print, it is very likely that the costs you are paying per interview or article is the cost of an ad plus a small mark up. Study the rates then find out what the cost of placing your own ad is. If the publicist is charging more, you might as well do it yourself.

In the end, always make sure you are comfortable with a company before you sign on any dotted lines. Trust your gut. It is your money.

A day in the life of a publicist

During a recent radio interview I was asked what a typical day as a publicist is for me. For the most part, it is a day filled with emails and telephone calls.   Some parts are exciting like interacting with media personalities and working with authors from all walks of life. Other parts are extremely draining such as hearing "no" every day.

First thing in the morning, I turn on my computer and start up my email program. Some days I only have about 30 new messages waiting for me. Other days I have hundreds of emails to wade through.   I respond to author inquiries, media interview or information requests, radio guest pitches, professional organization notifications and more. If any emails are requesting a review copy of a book, I create the press package and put it in the mail pile. I typically spend an hour trying to catch up each morning as more emails trickle in.

Next, I look at my clients' campaign calendars and determine which tasks I need to do each day. If I need to contact a targeted media group for an author, I compile that list of media and send out emails. If I need to set up events for an author, I start calling bookstores, libraries and other venues. Any media contacts that haven't responded by email I call to make my story pitch.

Sometimes I spend hours researching new media to contact. Media rarely stay in the same job for more than a couple of years. Maintaining my list of where people are and what they like to cover takes many hours.

The hardest part of my job is voicemail and hearing no. I invest myself emotionally into each project I take on. I want to get coverage for all of my authors and it is discouraging when a media contact isn't interested.

At the end of the day, I send off my last emails, grab my pile of mail to drop off at the post office and go home to my family. Some days I am energized because I arranged an appearance on national television for a client. Other days are draining when no one is interested in talking to my clients.

What I love about my job is being creative and figuring out different topics and angles to pitch to media. Every day is a little different because every author and every book is different.

Types of Publicity

There are many types of publicity. There is face-to-face publicity where you interact with people one-on-one. There is print and Internet media where your name, face and cover are seen. There is broadcast media where you are heard and/or seen interacting with a host. These all have a place in a well-rounded publicity campaign.

No matter what kind of publicity you want, there are four things you need for a successful campaign; a marketing plan, pre-publication publicity, press materials and review copies.

Marketing Plan

Would you try to drive to Alaska without a map? The odds are you won't make it to your destination in the time frame you want. It is quicker and more efficient to use a map. The same concept holds for publicity. There are several key points you need to outline. Those points you need to identify are your target audience, the media outlets whom cater to your target audience and the hooks you will use.

Section 3: Publicity

Your target audience is the people most likely to purchase your book. If you wrote a romance novel, your best market is women. If you wrote a book titled "C++ Demystified" you want to reach computer programming enthusiasts. Identify the portions of the population you think will find value in your writing.

After figuring out who you want to reach, the next step is to figure out who caters to that audience. Better Homes and Gardens typically isn't interested in the usual computer manual. You're better off contacting PCs R Us or something similar to cover that topic. Rush Limbaugh is not going to interview the author of a Harlequin Romance Novel and CNN won't cover the newest passing teen-fad. Choose your media carefully.

Finding media nationwide is a very time consuming task. Finding the contact information for the decision makers takes even longer. This is definitely one place where it benefits you to talk to a publicist. Most publicists have databases of contacts and can search by interest.

Another vital part of creating the marketing plan is to brainstorm who you want to endorse your book. You need to think about who has a big name in the industry you are writing for, which big name authors might enjoy your book, or people who have impressive titles. You spend the marketing portion of your book gathering contact information for those people.

Once you have your target audience and the target media, you must refine your hooks to catch your audience's interest so they want to interview you. You will have a different hook for every target audience and each media outlet that caters to that target audience. Sometimes you have to refine and re-refine your pitch several times until it is right.

Another vital part of creating a marketing plan is to set a monetary budget for your marketing actions. Determine how much money you can afford to lose, where it is coming from and where you will spend it. If you do this step, you will decrease the chance that you will go deep into debt and lose your house like some authors have done.

When I say plan how much you can afford to lose I say it that way to make sure you understand that publishing is a game of chance. You might not make your money back so do not spend more than you can afford to lose. Do not dedicate your mortgage payment to paying for a publicist. Do not use your food budget to buy bookmarks. Avoid tapping to your retirement, maxing out your credit cards or re-mortgaging your home to pay for publishing services.

Section 3: Publicity

Where is the money to pay for your publicity and marketing coming from? If you will use a little bit from each paycheck, plan out when you are paying for services. If you have money in a savings account, money market account, or CD you are using, consider how much you are really losing from compound interest. Make sure the risk is worth the investment.

If you are using a credit card, how much can you afford to pay each month? How much will your investment cost with interest by the time you have it paid off? Do not figure book sales into your calculations. When you are planning, you need to plan keeping in mind that your book sales might not cover the credit card payment each month. How long will it take you to pay off your investment using your existing income?

What supplies and services do you plan on purchasing? Do you like the idea of giving out pens? Do you want to give out bookmarks? You can give away shirts, bracelets, stuffed animals, brochures, key chains, clips, and more! You can get as creative as you want when developing marketing materials. You need to ask yourself if the cost of each item is worth the investment to sell your book or your services.

A solid marketing plan should be in depth and thorough. This part only covers a couple of the basics. For a more in depth guide to creating a marketing plan, consider taking an online course. I also have a marketing plan book in development to be released in 2011.

Section 3: Publicity

Writing a Killer Hook

Getting and keeping a media's attention can be a daunting task. They are inundated with hundreds, if not thousands, of Emails everyday from publicists, agents and individuals who want to get media coverage. You need to stand out from the rest of the messages destined for the trash bin. You can break out of the pack by crafting an amazing hook that reaches out and grabs your audience by the nose hairs!

Here are my top 20 hints for writing a hook.

1. **Tie into Current Events in the Media:** Watch and read the news and see what they are talking about. Find a way to put a unique spin on the story with your expertise. When the Hudson River emergency plane landing happened, one of my clients was contacted by Fox News almost immediately because the media discovered his book about a similar crash in 1974 online. Be aware of breaking events and contact media *immediately* if you can tie in to the story with a unique spin.

2. **How To:** Everyone likes to learn new things. Have your hook explain what the reader/viewer/listener will learn. For example, *Grab Em by the Nose Hairs! How to Get and Keep Media's Attention* is the media hook I would use.

3. **Top 10 (or any number):** Everyone knows about Dave and his famous Top Ten list. How many times have you seen a magazine with a big hook on the cover reading, "Top 10 Things to Drive Your Man Wild" or "5 Best Belly Fat Busting Tips"? In our society of too much information coming too fast, people like the most important facts filtered out for them and presented in an easy, quick list.

4. **Create a Holiday:** You can actually create your own official holidays. Make one that ties into your theme. Visit www.mhprofessional.com and register a date. If you don't want to go through the process of creating your own holiday, there is probably already one that you can tie into your theme! For example, just the month of October has all these holidays:

Produce, Publish, Publicize

a. Child Health Day
b. Nuclear Medicine Week begins (Oct 5-11)
c. Portugal: Republic Day
d. United Nations: World Habitat Day
e. United Nations: World Teachers' Day
f. Adopt-A-Shelter-Dog Month
g. Animal Safety and Protection Month, Natl
h. Antidepressant Death Awareness Month
i. Bake and Decorate Month, Natl
j. Breast Cancer Awareness Month, Natl
k. Celebrating the Bilingual Child Month
l. Celiac Disease Awareness Month
m. Children's Magazine Month
n. Chili Month, Natl
o. Chiropractic Month, Natl
p. Church Library Month
q. Church Safety and Security Month
r. Class Reunion Month
s. Co-op Awareness Month
t. Crime Prevention Month, Natl
u. Cyber Security Awareness Month, Natl
v. Dental Hygiene Month, Natl
w. Depression Education and Awareness Month, Natl
x. Disability Employment Awareness Month, Natl
y. Domestic Violence Awareness Month
z. Down Syndrome Awareness Month, Natl

aa. Dyslexia Awareness Month
bb. Eat Better, Eat Together Month
cc. Emotional Intelligence Awareness Month
dd. Emotional Wellness Month
ee. Family Sexuality Education Month, Natl
ff. "Gain the Inside Advantage" Month, Natl
gg. Gay and Lesbian History Month
hh. German-American Heritage Month
ii. Global Diversity Awareness Month
jj. Go Hog Wild--Eat Country Ham Month
kk. Go on a Field Trip Month, Natl
ll. Halloween Safety Month
mm.　Health Literacy Month
nn. Liver Awareness Month, Natl
oo. Long Term Care Planning Month
pp. Medical Librarians Month, Natl
qq. Month of Freethought
rr. Organize Your Medical Information Month
ss. Orthodontic Health Month, Natl
tt. Photographer Appreciation Month
uu. Physical Therapy Month, Natl
vv. Polish-American Heritage Month
ww. Popcorn Poppin' Month, Natl
xx. Positive Attitude Month
yy. Raptor Month
zz. Reading Group Month, Natl
aaa. Rett Syndrome Awareness Month

bbb. Right-Brainers Rule Month
ccc. Roller Skating Month, Natl
ddd. RSV Awareness Month, Natl
eee. Sarcastics Awareness Month, Natl
fff. Self-Promotion Month
ggg. Spina Bifida Awareness Month, Natl
hhh. Spinach Lovers Month
iii. Squirrel Awareness Month
jjj. Stamp Collecting Month, Natl
kkk. Starman Month, Intl
lll. Strategic Planning Month, Intl
mmm. Talk about Prescriptions Month
nnn. Vegetarian Month
ooo. Women's Small Business Month
ppp. Work and Family Month, Natl
qqq. Workplace Politics Awareness

5. **Play on Words:** Most people enjoy a good pun. If your last name is Wright, you can play on words by having your hook be "Learn to Fish the Wright Way!" Find someway to play around with words so that it sticks in a reader/listener/viewer's head.

6. **Challenge:** Everyone likes a challenge. I remember listening to a local station that had a segment called Stump Stu or something similar.

The whole point was to call in and ask a question that the host could not answer. If you can create a challenge that will get listeners/ viewers/ readers to participate, you have a successful hook.

7. **Put Me to the Test:** There are a lot of segments about an expert helping someone with a problem then that person talking about how much (or little) help it was. Create a situation where you fix something, advise someone, teach someone etc. Make it something that everyone's talking about and which is easy to explain. For example, a network show was working on a 90 day dating challenge where they followed around a middle aged woman as she tried to find someone worth dating in her city. There was an expert who was put to the test to identify which potential males would make the cut. Dating, finances, home design, phobias, and skills are all examples of areas that have potential.

8. **Tie to a Celebrity:** Actor Michael J. Fox has Parkinson's disease. If your book or platform has anything to do with Parkinson's, mentioning Michael J. Fox is a good big name to tie into. I worked on a book for tweens dealing with global warming and tied the hook into Former Vice

President and Environmentalist Al Gore since he is forefront in media's mind regarding global warming topics. Autism topics warrant a reference to Jenny McCarthy if you encourage holistic methods. Figure out which celebrities talk about or deal with your subject and look for tie-ins.

9. **Suggest Other People to Involve:** It might seem counter-productive to suggest that a media contact use someone else but you are communicating to the media that you really want to help them find sources to the point of offering someone else. This helps you get on the media contact's good list and that will start coming to you when they need information about your topic.

10. **Publicity Stunt:** Remember when basketball star Dennis Rodman said he was getting married? The media went into a frenzy that the NBA bad-boy was settling down with a mystery woman. At the set date and time, Dennis walked out of a limo – wearing a wedding gown. The whole thing was a publicity stunt. You may not want something as sensational but announcing that you are unveiling something special and keeping what a secret can be an effective publicity stunt if it's implied to help people with something they care about.

11. **Involve the Audience:** Producers love doing stunts that involve the audience. If you can think of something that will get listeners calling in, viewers jumping off their couches, the audience in the studio up and moving and interested or readers responding, you have a concept that producers want.

12. **Involve the Host:** People love the hosts getting involved as well. Think about the classic Johnny Carson shows where the guest is a zoo keeper with some animals and the animals end up all over Johnny. Those are classic, loved shows. How can you get the host involved?

13. **Hazards to Avoid:** Are you aware of a danger that most people don't think twice about? For example, if you are in the shoveling business and you discover that most people slip on ice because they forget to throw salt by the driver side door of the car, you can probably get some attention in the winter from media. You can offer articles, interviews and tips. If you know of something in your industry, contact media to warn their audience.

14. **Talk about a Problem:** There are problems that people talk about all the time. For instance, Health Care Reform is a huge topic everywhere at the moment. If you are informed and can talk about a problem intelligently, you can get interviews.

15. **Trends:** Media contacts like to report about something first. If you notice a trend in society or your area, talk about it to the media. For example, a huge trend right now is Social Media. Social Media is using online networking sites to meet new clients, make sales and grow your business. Customers want close personal access to you and Social Media is the modern way to cater to that need. Social Media is a trend that most media outlets talk about.

16. **Make-Over:** Offer a make over. If you have a service or product that helps people, offer to make someone over for free (which media can use as a contest or award making them look better). The ongoing success of Extreme Makeover: Home Edition is one example of the potential for success.

17. **Time of Year:** Do you have a book about Winter Time activities? Your best bet is to pitch this topic in late fall to media. When a season, date or holiday is coming up that relates to your book,

contact as many media as possible as fast as possible before that season.

18. **Controversial Issue:** There are many controversial issues that people continue to talk about. Abortion, race issues, politics, health care reform and religion are some basic ones. In my industry, self publishing versus commercial publishing is a huge controversial issue that comes up often.

19. **Promote Failure:** Have you tried something 100 times and failed? Then on the 101st time you got it? People love inspirational stories about someone who tries and tries and tries and finally overcomes their trial.

20. **Create a Great Name:** Call yourself something that is catchy. If you have seen *Confessions of a Shopaholic*, the main character calls herself the girl in the green scarf. An author I worked with was one of the Dixie Divas. If you have a fail proof way to win the lottery, call yourself the Payout King/Queen. Use that name for yourself to create your platform and promote your title.

The bottom line is you need to think of a great way to get attention in the first 10 seconds. No matter how well written your press release is, it doesn't do you any good if your audience throws it away or deletes your email message without reading it.

Section 3: Publicity

Pre-Publication Date Publicity

Have you noticed the blurbs on the front covers of best selling books? Ever wonder how an author gets those? It's through basic pre-publication publicity.

When you are published through a traditional publisher, several galleys or Advance Review Copies (ARCs) are sent out to the major book reviewers across the nation. The ARC is created from a manuscript that is almost completely done with editing but still about 3-4 months before the publication date. It is usually bound in book form and mailed off. The reviewers get first crack at it and send back comments and publish reviews in different media outlets close to your release date.

The publisher then picks which blurbs they like best and add it to the final cover art. Hopefully, the people you identified as potential endorsers send back feedback in addition to reviewers.

Advance Review Copies are a vital part of getting buzz before your release date. Once your publication date has passed, most large press book reviewers won't even consider a review.

Section 3: Publicity

Remember that media want to be the first to everything. Look at the word news. The first three letters spell new. If you are contacting large media outlets and your book is already released and has no tie to a current event, you will usually be ignored.

Spend the months before your release date researching media and contacting them for reviews, articles, features and interviews on your topics. If you can offer them the chance to be the first to talk about your subject, they will appreciate the courtesy.

Press Materials

A good publicity campaign will always have press materials created before a single media member is contacted. In my company we consider a press release, a sell sheet, a Q&A and two cover letters essential for a publicity campaign.

The press release is one page that describes the book in approximately 4 paragraphs, contains one paragraph about the author and the bottom line contains the publishing information about the book. The publishing information includes the size of the book, the ISBN, the publication date and the cover price.

The sell sheet is created for bookstores only. It announces the publishing details of the book in a concise manner with a small area for the book specifics.

The Q&A is for media that might consider an interview. The Q&A consists of approximately 2 pages of questions and the answers. The questions are pertinent to the book's topics and the author fills in the answers in a conversational manner. This gives the interviewer ideas for questions to ask and the answers to expect.

The cover letters have 2-3 paragraphs each that are focused to a particular topic discussed in the book. The intent of a cover letter is to catch the media contact's attention and interest him or her enough to read the press release.

Anyone can attempt to write their own press materials but I have seen many poorly written ones created by well meaning authors. There are market standards that need to be integrated in each page that people in the industry know. Even a publicist like me working in the field for years has someone else writing my press kits for my clients. I recommend you hire a book publicity firm to write your materials. Expect to pay $200.00 or more for a complete set.

Review Copies

To garner publicity, you need to send review copies to people to read. You may end up with some reviewers writing about you because they purchased your book but for the most part, you will need to send a free copy. Depending on your publisher they may provide all of your review copies and take care of sending them to reviewers.

Of course the large and small commercial publishers will be sending out review copies months in advance of your release. With vanity presses you may have 50 free copies to send to reviewers. Other vanity publishers require you to purchase every copy of your book. The bottom line is if you aren't published with a commercial publisher, expect to send review copies.

The review copies may be sent to print, online and broadcast media. Who you actually send to depends on your marketing plan.

Face-to-Face Publicity

Marketing experts might call face-to-face publicity direct marketing instead of a publicity tactic. I call it micro-publicity because you never know who has an audience. For example, one person might have over 1,000 dedicated readers or friends. If impressing that one person means 1,000 people will know about you or your product, is that person any less valuable as a media contact than a community newspaper editor? Social Media has turned the majority of our population into independent media outlets.

Face-to-face publicity can include telling your friends and family about your book, talking to complete strangers while waiting in line at the grocery store, or doing a book signing. You are the best sales-person for your book because you have the most vested interest in its success.

Some of the most successful authors carry copies of his or her book in the trunk of their car on the off chance someone might express interest in buying a copy. This eliminates the chance of losing a sale to short attention spans or poor memory.

Also, if you are published through a vanity press, you probably make a better profit selling the books in person as opposed to Amazon.com or in a book store.

Book Signings

Book signings are a very popular way to publicize your book face-to-face. A book signing is typically at a bookstore but can be anywhere you choose. A bookstore is the optimal location because there is always the potential to interest random book lovers in your book without paying for advertising or renting a location. Also most bookstores have a mailing list to tell their customers about upcoming events. This equates to free publicity!

If you set a book signing up somewhere other than a bookstore, you are solely responsible finding and possibly renting the location and for letting the people know about your event. It is in an author's best interest to look for a bookstore first.

The bad news: Bookstores are beginning to avoid author events unless the author is someone like Stephen King. An event takes a lot of time, expense and preparation for the bookstores and unfortunately, book signings are losing popularity unless it is for a major personality. Even then, major personalities have been known to have book signings that have five people show up in four hours.

At the time of this writing I just heard from different Barnes and Noble locations that they only host events with authors approved by the national office. This is not good news for any author who chooses or is tricked into publishing with a vanity press. It is very difficult for a vanity press author to be approved by the national office.

The first items a bookstore considers when deciding whether to host you, as an unknown author, are: return status, cover price and local tie. There are some stores that will overlook a high cover price or possibly even the return status but if you have a bad answer to all of those items, it will be hard to secure events.

Return Status:

Bookstores want to be able to return your book to the distributor. If they cannot return your book to the distributor, the large chain stores are generally going to turn your book event down. Always find out the answer to this question before signing a contract with a publisher. If you don't know if your title is returnable or not after you have published, a bookstore will be able to tell you.

There are some exceptions so if you know you aren't returnable to the distributor, ask if the location will consider a consignment based signing. A consignment signing means you as the author will bring your own copies of your book and sell them through the bookstore's cash register or you will bring a cash box to make change. If you sell through their cash register, after the signing (sometimes weeks after the signing), you will receive a check for your percentage of the total revenue generated from the signing. Any unsold books you left with the store will be returned to you at that time.

Section 3: Publicity

Cover Price:

Because some Print-on-Demand companies will allow returns through the distributor now, bookstores have been adjusting how they can tell if a book is Print-on-Demand and marketable. Looking at the cover price is one of those methods. If the cover price isn't competitive, chances are you aren't going to sell many books even with a book signing.

Bookstores know the average cost of books. Because you followed my advice in the publishing section, your book will be in the proper price range and you won't have a problem with this part.

If you did not read this book before publishing and you have a high cover price it does not mean you will always be turned down for a signing. Always ask.

Local Tie:

Unless you can prove you have a big following all over the nation, many bookstores will only consider hosting you if you are local. Book events don't typically bring in a big crowd without a strong local tie for a first time author.

Most new authors can plan on friends and family attending their signing and not many more people. This does not mean a local book signing is going to be a waste of time. The author should consider it a time to celebrate with friends and family and the opportunity to talk to new people.

The goal of a book signing is not to make thousands of dollars in one night. The whole point is for people to get to know you and find nice things to say about you. Word-of-mouth is still the most effective publicity in existence.

Best-Selling Hopeful

Your large traditional publishing house will set up book signings for you in your local area as well as nationwide either through an in-house publicity agent or a contract publicity agent as fits in the publicity budget.

Your publisher may not send you all over the

world for signings. It will depend on the marketing plan and budget for your title.

If you received an advance, consider investing that money into arranging and traveling to more book events than what your publisher arranged.

Make-a-Buck

Depending on whom you published through, your publisher might set book signings up for you or you might be on your own. You are capable of setting up a book signing without help but depending on how much free time you have, you might consider getting help from a publicist.

Posterity Writer

What a better way to celebrate your works than with a local author event? I think one author event set up and announced to friends and family is a great way to celebrate together. More than one event will tax your friends and family. Since you're not writing for anyone else, that's all you want there. You may consider hosting a bash at your house or local church instead of a bookstore if you get a better deal from your publisher by ordering directly and reselling.

Many bookstores want to know that you have a publicity campaign set up so the general public knows about the event. This means that all the media is aware of your event and you are listed on several calendars of events. It's also a good idea to get as many interviews as possible to further promote your work.

You have the ability to do this all this yourself but you might also consider hiring a publicist to assist you. A publicist gives you credibility, takes all the rejection for you and should have access to contact information you are not privy to.

In the event where you do not have access to a publicist for whatever reason and you choose to promote yourself, use the following worksheets to guide you in setting up book events.

Book Signing Check List

My book is returnable. (circle one) Yes No

Top 10 Bookstores I want to host an event:
Name   Telephone Number
1. _____
2. _____
3. _____
4. _____
5. _____
6. _____
7. _____
8. _____
9. _____
10. _____

You don't have to fill every line if your community does not have many bookstores close to you. Just have several options listed here to make it easier to keep calling even if you receive a "no."

Look at your calendar for a month or two ahead. If it's currently March, look at the end of April, all of May and June. Figure out which dates absolutely do not work for you and cross those dates off. Then call the bookstores on your list above and ask for a signing. If you are calling

B&N, ask for their CRM (Community Relations Manager). Ask other stores for the manager in charge of author events.

Schedule your event for a month or more in the future. This gives the location time to include the announcement of your event in their newsletter and gives you time to set up interviews and articles announcing your upcoming events.

Enter the information for each signing on the next few pages.

Event 1:

Date:_____ Time:_____ AM/PM

Location:_____

_____

Contact Person:_____

Telephone:_____

Bookmarks: ☐ Requested   ☐ Sent

Poster: ☐ Requested   ☐ Sent

Section 3: Publicity

Event 2:

Date:_____Time:_____AM/PM

Location:_____

_____

Contact Person:_____

Telephone:_____

Bookmarks: ☐ Requested   ☐ Sent

Poster: ☐ Requested   ☐ Sent

Event 3:

Date:_____Time:_____AM/PM

Location:_____

_____

Contact Person:_____

Telephone:_____

Bookmarks: ☐ Requested   ☐ Sent

Poster: ☐ Requested   ☐ Sent

Produce, Publish, Publicize

Event 4:

Date:_____Time:_____AM/PM

Location:_____

_____

Contact Person:_____

Telephone:_____

Bookmarks: ☐ Requested   ☐ Sent

Poster: ☐ Requested   ☐ Sent

Event 5:

Date:_____Time:_____AM/PM

Location:_____

_____

Contact Person:_____

Telephone:_____

Bookmarks: ☐ Requested   ☐ Sent

Poster: ☐ Requested   ☐ Sent

Section 3: Publicity

Event 6:

Date:_____Time:_____AM/PM

Location:_____

_____

Contact Person:_____

Telephone:_____

Bookmarks: ☐ Requested   ☐ Sent

Poster: ☐ Requested   ☐ Sent

Event 7:

Date:_____Time:_____AM/PM

Location:_____

_____

Contact Person:_____

Telephone:_____

Bookmarks: ☐ Requested   ☐ Sent

Poster: ☐ Requested   ☐ Sent

Event 8:

Date:_____Time:_____AM/PM

Location:_____

_____

Contact Person:_____

Telephone:_____

Bookmarks: ☐ Requested   ☐ Sent

Poster: ☐ Requested   ☐ Sent

Event 9:

Date:_____Time:_____AM/PM

Location:_____

_____

Contact Person:_____

Telephone:_____

Bookmarks: ☐ Requested   ☐ Sent

Poster: ☐ Requested   ☐ Sent

Section 3: Publicity

Event 10:

Date:_____Time:_____AM/PM

Location:_____

_____

Contact Person:_____

Telephone:_____

Bookmarks: ☐ Requested   ☐ Sent

Poster: ☐ Requested   ☐ Sent

Bookmarks and Posters

The bookmarks and posters are very important parts of promoting yourself. I suggest leaving 30-60 bookmarks and a poster one month in advance for each book signing location. The bookstore will typically put the bookmarks on the front counter and let customers take them. It's great free advertising for them and it's a minimal investment for the author. If you are computer savvy, you can make them up rather quickly. I shoot for 5 bookmarks on a full page when I'm advertising an event. For generic bookmarks, I shoot for 20 bookmarks on a page.

On the following page, I have laid out a sample bookmark. Notice the cover image is on the bookmark. You want people to know which book they want to buy by sight. The title and the author's name is also listed below the book in case the writing on your cover ends up too small to read. This avoids any confusion. There is also an advertisement for the event listed. You may opt to put a very short book summation here instead but I find an advertisement for the event more effective when you have a book signing to advertise. On the back, have short blurbs praising your book. Since you have this guide, you know pre-publicity is key to a successful campaign and have already gathered endorsements before setting up your event!

Bookmark Front   **Bookmark Back**

Author Event

PRODUCE,
PUBLISH,
PUBLICIZE:

What every writer should know to create an
amazing book, avoid publishing traps and
scams as well as increase sales.

SABRINA
SUMSION

Meet the author
Sabrina Sumsion
here at
Barnes and Noble
South Point
Pavilions
Lincoln, NE

December 11, 2010
at
6:59PM

"Reading this book saved me thousands of dollars when I published my book!"
-Joe Schmoe, author

"I have never read anything that will prepare an author more for publishing."
-Jane Smith, author

"We need more information! Sabrina, keep it coming! It's easy to understand, all books should be written this way."
-John Wright, author

"There is no easy way to summarize how great this book is. If you are even remotely interested in publishing a book, make sure to read Produce, Publish, Publicize cover to cover!"
-Frank Rider, author

Section 3: Publicity

Now that you have your bookmarks designed, print the bookmarks on nice glossy paper. I have found that photo paper is durable and it looks more professional than regular printer paper. Cardstock would be another option for an author doing bookmarks him or her self who does not want gloss. If you watch your local Target-type stores, you can find packs of 100 sheets of durable paper on sale for $10.00. You can also find it on the Internet inexpensively.

You want a nice printer to print the bookmarks. If your printer leaves lines or a grainy look, consider going to Kinkos or another printing shop. Last I checked, Kinkos charges $0.50 per color sheet. For 30 large bookmarks, you'll pay $3.00.

There are also many companies online that will print bookmarks for you if you don't want to make your own. Do a google search for "buy bookmarks" and you will find many options ranging in all sizes.

If you intend to hold several author events I do encourage you to get a large poster of your book cover or another image to advertise your presence. There are a few places online where you can order a large poster for around $15.00. To get a nice large poster you need to be prepared with a very large image with 600 or more dpi (dots per inch). Your cover designer will be able to provide this file for you.

Major publishers print out 2'x 3' or larger posters for the bookstores to display for each book signing depending on the budget. It probably won't be practical for an author doing their own publicity to create this size of poster for every signing as the odds are he or she won't make their money back from books sold at the event. A simple 8 1/2" x 11" sheet is sufficient for getting the information out in that situation.

The poster should always start with what you are advertising. The next thing is where, followed by when. These are the most vital parts of the poster. Without this information, this poster is worthless to the reader. The middle part of the poster is advertising filler. It gives more information to the reader as to the topic and relevance. The last line should always be an invitation. Invite the reader to the event in a way to interest them. In the example on the next page, the interest hook is saving money. That appeals to most people.

BOOK SIGNING

Right here with:
SABRINA SUMSION

December 11, at 7PM

What readers are saying:
"**I wish I had read this book before publishing.** It would have saved me so many headaches!

-John Doe, author of Secrets Revealed

Produce, Publish, Publicize is a how-to guide for avoiding the publishing industry's dirtiest traps and scams. You will learn how to increase your chances for publicity and sales. Written by a publicist who was saddened every time she had to break the reality of the publishing world to starry-eyed authors duped into publishing with less than reputable sources and using lack-luster editing services, this guide contains the information you need to increase your chances of success!

Join Sabrina right here for an informational night that will save you thousands of dollars!

Print Media

Now that you have a book signing or two lined up for a month or more in the future, it's time to start contacting print media. Print media can include newspapers and magazines. Newspapers and especially magazines need a lot of lead time because of editorial constraints and printing deadlines.

Print media publicity can come in the form of a review, an interview or a simple announcement of an event based around your book. The most ideal is an interview. This will give readers a connection to you that garners loyalty. Interviews based on an author's work aren't very common in larger newspapers except for established personalities. Smaller communities may have the editorial space for a first time author.

A review of your book is always good publicity. Typically, you will need to send a free copy of your book to a reviewer to get the review published.

An announcement for your event or two is beneficial to get. These are typically printed in a

Section 3: Publicity

calendar of events section of newspapers and sometimes magazines. These let people know what is going on and should never be turned down.

Contacting Print Media

To contact print media, as an author, you have a few ways of figuring out how to get a hold of the correct person. The first I suggest is looking through the paper or magazine you want to be featured in and finding the names of the people writing the articles about your book's topic. Try to find out who is in charge of the features section or the book reviews section. Usually at the end of an article, the writer's contact information is published. Get a list together of all the people you want to contact before you start contacting so you don't accidentally duplicate your efforts.

You also have the option of contacting a publicity firm and purchasing media contacts that are targeted to your book. Not all publicity firms sell the contact names and if they do, they typically will not do a full publicity campaign for the same book after selling those names. Publicists do not like to waste time re-contacting media and they want to maintain positive professional relationships with those media contacts.

Email:

Email is the easiest way to initially contact media. You can reach several people and you don't have to worry about time zones and if they are at work or not. The message is in their inbox and when they have time they will read it.

Media have spam blockers so watch your inbox carefully for Emails asking you to authenticate you are a real person and not a spam machine. Always reply to those messages. You may be asked to remove a media's contact information from your contact list. Do not take it personally. These people get hundreds of contacts a day and sometimes don't take the time to figure out they really are interested. Simply remove them from your list and move on to the next contact.

The format of the Email you send should be along these lines:

(*begin outline*)
Subject Line:New <couple words describing your book> book for your consideration

Body:
<Cover letter>
<Signature>

<Press release>

(*end outline*)

The press release Email I sent to print media for *Produce, Publish, Publicize* reads along these lines:

Subject Line:New guide for writers for your consideration

(*cover letter*)
Hi <Contact First Name>!

Section 3: Publicity

Following please find press materials for the new publishing guide, *Produce, Publish, Publicize*, by literary publicist Sabrina Sumsion.

Did you know that 83% of the American adult population dreams of being an author? More and more people are publishing books but unfortunately many of these people's literary dreams are turning into publishing nightmares. Authors are under educated and taken advantage of to the tune of thousands of dollars.

Produce, Publish, Publicize is a how-to guide for developing a professional product, avoiding the publishing industry's dirtiest traps and scams then increasing sales. *Produce, Publish, Publicize* is written by a literary publicist saddened every time she had to break the reality of the publishing world to starry eyed-authors duped into publishing with less than reputable sources. This guide contains the information every writer needs to increase their chances of successfully publishing!

Please contact me if you would like a review copy of *Produce, Publish, Publicize,* are interested in Sabrina writing a guest article for your publication or if you would like to interview Sabrina.

Thank You,

Sabrina Sumsion
<Company> (optional)
<Telephone number>
<Email address>

(*Press release in the same Email as the cover letter but below the signature*)
FOR IMMEDIATE RELEASE
Contact: Sabrina Sumsion
<Company> (optional)
<Telephone number>
<Email address>

In her new guide on the literary industry, *Produce, Publish, Publicize*, Sabrina Sumsion attempts to educate the reader on the traps and scams involved in becoming an author. This new book contains vital information for any aspiring author!

Some of the topics Produce, Publish, Publicize covers are:
- How to create a professional product
- What publishing avenues are available and the

benefits and drawbacks to each
■   What every author can do to publicize his or her books with or without a publicist.

Produce, Publish, Publicize acknowledges that not all authors set out to be best sellers. What may be good for one author may not be good for another. Each section speaks to the three main groups of authors and advises them each step of the way.

With more and more authors dissatisfied by their publishing experience, this book is the guide the writing industry has been waiting for.

About the author:
Sabrina Sumsion hosts a radio show discussing a wide variety of publishing and publicity topics ranging from choosing a publisher to getting media's attention to marketing tips for authors. An experienced publicist, she has worked on a broad variety of campaigns such as Michael Wilkinson's *Masterful Meetings* and Adam Shepard's *Scratch Beginnings*. For more details about Sabrina, please visit www.sabrinasumsion.com.

978-0-9824126-0-2 * May 2010 * 8 x 5 Paperback * 12.95

(*End of Email*)

The goal is for the cover letter to entice the media contact to keep reading and find out more about the book. The press release has more information about the book and is intended to convince the media contact they want to read the book or do a review. At that point, hopefully the media contact will request a review copy.

Section 3: Publicity

Creating a Press Kit

Your amazing Email to print media generated interest and now you have a review copy request. It is time to print out and send a professional press kit. A nice folder in a color that co-ordinates with your book's color scheme should hold your press materials. For a press kit to media, I put an individualized cover letter in front then the press release behind it on the left hand inner pocket. In the right inner pocket, I put the Q&A sheets.

For a press kit to a bookstore, I put an individualized cover letter in front and the press release behind it in the left-hand pocket. On the right side, I put a sell sheet. I always make sure to have my contact information plastered everywhere so they can get a hold of me again. I have at least one contact method on each page if not 2-3 contact methods.

I also include a business card with every review copy I send out. I also put a professional sticker outlining the title, author, genre, publication date and my contact information on the cover of my review copy. This reduces the chance that the reviewers will sell the book and it increases the chance that they will find my information to contact me.

Once I have the press kit compiled, I send it Priority Mail with my review copy. The reason for Priority Mail is media have short attention spans. You want to get your book in the media's hand as soon as possible. If you use www.usps.com to print out your shipping label, you get free delivery confirmation as well as a reduced rate.

Three business days after mailing your press kit, call or Email the media contact and make sure they received the press kit. If they didn't, track the package and make sure it arrived at their door. Sometimes Priority Mail takes more than 3 days. Other times, the book arrived but was lost in the nether world of the mail department. Wait a couple more business days and if they still haven't seen your package, it's easiest to send another. Yes, you just lost a book but you really want the review or interview more, right?

If the media contact received the book, ask if they have any questions then assure them they can contact you at anytime for more information.

Now the hard part is waiting to see if the media contact will do anything with your book. Print media can take upwards of two months before they print anything. Stories featuring books and authors typically are filler and only used if there is a gap on a page. Be patient and wait a couple weeks at least before re-contacting a print media contact if they have not already gotten a hold of you. You don't want to annoy them especially when they are on a deadline so be patient.

Back to your list of remaining media contacts, if I don't hear from a media contact whether they are interested or not in a review copy, I do a follow up Email. In this Email, I simply do a cover letter letting the contact know I haven't heard from them and will be calling. The Email looks like:

Subject: Follow up to New guide for writers for your consideration

Hi <Contact Name>!

I haven't heard back from you on whether you would like a review copy of the new publishing guide *Produce, Publish, Publicize* or if you would like to set up an interview. Please let me know if I can put a review copy in the mail for you today! I will call in a couple of days to follow up if I haven't heard from you.

Just in case your spam filter caught my first

message, *Produce, Publish, Publicize* is a how-to guide for avoiding the publishing industry's dirtiest traps and scams. Writers will learn how to increase their chances for publicity and sales. *Produce, Publish, Publicize* is written by a publicist saddened every time she had to break the reality of the publishing world to starry-eyed authors duped into publishing with less than reputable sources. This guide contains the information every writer needs to increase their chances of successfully publishing!

Thank you for your time!

Sabrina Sumsion
<Company> (optional)
<Telephone number>
<Email address>

Usually this Email will get a response if that person is checking their Emails. If a media personality isn't interested, they do not want me calling so they will send back an Email saying no thank you.

If I do not get a response, the next step is to call. Sometimes my Email gets tangled in a spam filter or I have an old Email address so the media contact will only find out about the opportunity to review my book if I call them. Usually, the media contact wasn't interested and simply deleted my Email without responding. Sometimes, the media contact hasn't checked their Email or they simply haven't taken the time to request a review copy. By calling, I know one way or another.

I have outlined the steps for calling media for a pretend media contact. The contact is May Smith with Metropolis Post. She is the features editor and you have not heard back from her by Email.

1.   Call the number you have for the media contact and request that person. Media contacts change jobs frequently so this step is vital for your records to make sure you are Emailing the correct person. If that person no longer works at the company jump to 2.

a.   You get May's voicemail. Leave a succinct message introducing yourself, leaving your number twice and telling a little bit about the book.

Hi May! This is Sabrina Sumsion from Sumsion Publicity. My number is 402-484-8124. I am calling in regards to some Emails I have sent about the new publishing guide *Produce, Publish, Publicize*.

Produce, Publish, Publicize is a guide for anyone who is considering writing a book. It explains what types of publishers exist, how each type affects the marketability of their book, the traps to watch for and the questions to ask. It also gives insider tips on how to publicize a book. Since 83% of American adults dream of publishing a book and thousands of books are published each day, this is a timely work. Call me back and let me know if I can send you a review copy today. My number again is 402-484-8124. May, I look forward to hearing back from you. Have a great day!

b.   May answers the phone. Remember the hook on which you worked so diligently? Now is the time to have that ready. You need to catch that person's interest and get past the "Who cares?" factor.

i.   Introduce yourself: Hi May! My name is Sabrina Sumsion from Sumsion Publicity.

ii.   Ask if she saw the Emails from you: I

am calling to follow up on a couple of Emails I sent this week regarding the new publishing guide *Produce, Publish, Publicize*. Did you see those Emails? If the answer is no, skip to iii.

1. If they remember your Email, they will probably tell you right away if they are interested or not. If they ask for more information, explain –succinctly –your book, who it benefits and what a reader should learn from reading it.

   Produce, Publish, Publicize is a guide for anyone who is considering writing a book. It explains what types of publishers exist, how each type affects the marketability of their book, the traps to watch for and the questions to ask. It also gives insider tips on how to publicize a book. Since 83% of American adults dream of publishing a book and thousands of books are published each day, this is a timely work. Would you like a review copy?

   a.   If they say yes, verify their mailing address and the spelling of their name. Let them know you will be mailing them a review copy right away. Thank them for their time.

b. If they say no, thank them for their time and tell them to contact you at anytime if they need information about your topic. You always want to leave on a positive note and leave the door open to work with the contact in the future.

Thank you for your time May. If you ever need information about publishing or publicity, please give me a call right away and I would be delighted to assist you!

iii. May doesn't remember seeing your Email. This is not a completely horrible answer. Your Emails may have been caught by her spam filter, she accidentally hit Delete on your Emails as she was hurrying to empty her inbox or you might have the wrong Email address. Tell her succinctly about your book just like if she asked for more information.

Produce, Publish, Publicize is a guide for anyone who is considering writing a book. It explains what types of publishers exist, how each type affects the marketability of their book, the traps to watch for and the questions to ask. It also gives insider tips on how to publicize a book. Since 90% of American adults dream of publishing a book and thousands of books are published each day, this is a timely work. Would you like a review copy?

a. If they say yes, verify their mailing address and the spelling of their name. Let them know you will be mailing them a review copy right away. Thank them for their time.

b. If they say no, thank them for their time and tell them to contact you at any time if they need information about your topic. You always want to leave on a positive note and leave the door open to work with the contact in the future.

Thank you for your time May. If you ever need information about publishing or publicity, please give me a call right away and I would be delighted to assist you!

2. That person no longer works at the

media outlet. Look at the media contact's title. If the media contact's title was features editor, ask who the current features editor is. *Write that person's name down* and ask to speak with him or her. Then follow the outline above as if you were sent to the right person all along.

Calling media is sometimes intimidating. They might seem very unhappy or impatient on the phone. The media might be on a deadline you aren't aware of or they are just having a crummy day. If your media contact seems cold and curt on the telephone understand it's probably not you with whom they are upset. Always be kind, polite and brief on the phone.

Articles and Print Media

Many times I come across a print media whose sole reason for turning down a review copy is because they do not have the staff to write a review or discuss the topic. Because of this, I try to have a couple of articles prepared that I can offer the media to publish for free.

By offering the magazine a free article, it helps them by filling an open space in their editorial line up, lowers overhead because they do not have to pay a writer for the submission and also offers content they would like to offer their readers but simply do not have the time to generate in-house.

If I'm not getting paid for my submission, how does it help me? It helps me because I get to write a bio for the end of the article where I will plug the books I have written. I also gain credibility as an expert because I am published in a magazine on my topic.

Create an outline for an article on one topic to start. Create one version of 800 words and one version of 1200 words. This gives the magazine options when choosing where to place your article.

Section 3: Publicity

Always remember to write a short bio that has contact information, a blurb about your book as well as a little bit about your expertise.

The magazine may ask for a headshot or cover image as well. This does not mean any old image. This means they want a high resolution (lots of DPI –dots per inch) image for printing. The picture you have online is probably not a high enough quality. Magazines want a minimum of 300 DPI for a crisp, professional image. Your cover designer will have a high quality image so you can get it from him or her. For a headshot, you may need to get a photographer's assistance. You can arrange to get a professional photo shoot for a variety of amazing shots. If you just need an image fast, your local Walmart, JC Penney's or Sears might have a walk-in photo studio.

Always have these ready before you contact a magazine. They have deadlines and will not include you if they can't get what they need from you in a timely manner.

Best-Seller Hopeful
Your traditional publisher will arrange for all of your print media. Take the initiative and create a couple of articles for print media. You may have requests for more information and interview

requests to meet but the effort of finding media interested will not fall on your shoulders alone. Since you received an advance, consider investing in your book and hiring a private publicist, purchase media contact information for areas you are traveling to or compile your own list of media contacts.

Make-a-Buck

Depending on your publishing route, you may or may not need to arrange print media. Before you go with any publishing route, find out exactly what the publisher is going to do to promote your book. Because you want to make sales, you should consider hiring a publicist if you do not have several hours everyday to dedicate to promoting your book.

Posterity Authors

You may be interested in getting an interview from your local newspaper to put in a scrapbook for your posterity. If you are from a smaller community, it shouldn't be too hard to arrange. If you are from New York where every other house has an aspiring author it may be much harder to secure anything in print. I wouldn't spend money on a publicist to get that media attention as your target audience is rather small and you can reach them on your own.

Broadcast media

Broadcast media consists of radio and television. Radio is always a good option for authors and television is even better. Radio helps people hear your voice and hear your name. It is a great way to spend time talking about your subject. Television is better because people hear your voice, hear your name, hear abut your product and also *see* those things. Adding another sensory dimension helps the public remember your name.

For beginners in media though, I always recommend radio first. You can get your feet wet with interviews, hone your message as well as choose a relaxing setting to hold your interview.

Radio:

There are two different types of radio programs. There are local programs and syndicated programs. A local radio station has local personalities who usually host programs live but are sometimes taped. These stations broadcast to different sizes of areas all across the nation.

Syndicated programs are shows with major personalities hosting such as Sean Hannidy and

Delilah. These shows are taped and then sent to customer radio stations across the nation for airing. When a show becomes syndicated, a radio personality has reached the pinnacle of their career.

It is much easier to schedule an interview with a local program than it is to schedule one with a syndicated program. Top authors and personalities want to be on syndicated programs because they reach a broader audience so you are competing for air time with big fish. The right topic will get you on top radio shows but understand you really need a phenomenal hook.

Depending on the goal of the interview, you might want a local program more than a syndicated program. Local programs are great for letting people know about an event in their area. Syndicated programs are good for making a broad audience aware of your book.

Television:
Television is also divided into two sections. There is local television and network television. Local television covers local programming with a lot of purchased network shows.

Network television reaches millions of people at one time and is the optimal way to reach the broadest amount of consumers. It is very difficult to get on a network show.

One thing I regularly tell the authors I speak with is they are not going to be featured on Oprah. I don't say that to be mean. I simply am trying to give the author a reality check. I do tell them I will make every effort to contact Oprah's producers but more than likely I will never hear back from them. Now that Oprah has announced she is retiring, there is going to be a mad rush from people nationally and internationally vying for her attention.

This is a harsh reality for the majority of authors. There is the possibility for authors to be published through traditional publishing routes to secure a few minutes of Oprah's airtime but even then the possibility is slim. I would love to hear a vanity press author without a big name became an exception to the rule but I don't see it happening before Oprah retires.

When contacting the broadcast media, I use the same format as the print media. I Email them first with a similar cover letter and press kit. If I don't hear back, I call and see if they are interested in receiving a review copy or setting up an interview.

Sometimes the broadcast media is interested in an interview but wants to see your recorded presence first. If you are setting yourself up to be an expert on a subject, it is wise to have video of you presenting to an audience ready for television. Most fiction writers are not setting themselves up as experts so a video isn't necessary.

Best-Seller Hopeful

Your traditional publisher will arrange for all of your broadcast media. Your publisher will finance any costs to have an interview with broadcast media whether it be traveling expenses or a meal budget. Even though your publisher is taking on the costs, it never hurts to invest your advance in publicity as well. There are thousands of contacts that change each year and a second person working the phones can deliver results.

Make-a-Buck

Depending on your publishing route, you may or may not need to arrange broadcast media for yourself. This is a great avenue for you to get into but television is hard to arrange if you are a fiction writer.

Do put forth the effort for radio stations at least. There are thousands of general interest shows nationwide you can contact for interviews. There are also hundreds if not thousands of shows dedicated to a broad range of topics. Do an Internet

search or contact a publicist to find shows that fit
your book's topic.

Posterity Authors

You may be interested in getting an interview
from your local radio or television station since you
aren't planning on selling hundreds of copies, don't
be overly concerned with gaining publicity. The
people who matter to you will know you developed
a book when you call them up and tell them.

Section 3: Publicity

Internet

Odds are, you have heard of the Internet. Maybe you use it, maybe you don't. You may use Email to stay in contact with family or send and receive business messages, you may surf the web, you may Facebook or Myspace regularly. No matter what your familiarity with the Internet is, it is one of the most powerful, yet misunderstood, publicity tools you can have.

The basics:
The Internet is simply millions of computers connected and sharing information. You send information from your computer and the information jumps from computer to computer until it reaches its destination. This is a very basic explanation of the Internet but the point is the information travels across paths from computer to computer to reach you.

How do I get started on the Internet?
The easiest place to start on the Internet is getting an Email address. Currently, my favorite

Email provider is Gmail. They provide free Email accounts and the program is easy to use. You can create an account at www.gmail.com. There are other companies such as Yahoo, Hotmail and local Internet service providers.

To get a small taste of the Internet, send some Emails to friends and family. This is a safe way to get a taste of the ease of communication the Internet provides.

I have Email, what's next?

For publicity purposes, you want to arrange a website next. You want a place where people who have heard of you or your books can go to find out more information, buy a book, ask questions or leave comments and suggestions.

You have a couple of options for getting a website on the Internet. You can use a free service that provides a limited number of templates, learn HTML and CSS and build your own or you can hire an outside company to build one for you.

Free services

A simple Google search for free website revealed hundreds of companies willing to host a website for you for free. Some of them require that ads are shown on your pages. Some of them are harvesting contact information to sell to spammers. Others want to sell you side services such as domain registration. Still others offer a free edition to entice you to upgrade to their premier service (which is not free).

These free services can be what you are looking for if your needs are very basic. You are limited by their provided templates and color schemes. This may or may not be a problem depending upon your project. The price is certainly easy to fit into your budget!

Learn html and CSS and build your own website
If you are interested in computers and have the time to learn how to program, building your own website might appeal to you. In this case, there are online tutorials that teach HTML and CSS as well as volumes of books dedicated to the subject.

You will need a webhost as well as a domain name. The webhost is the server (dedicated computer) that will hold your website files, run 24/7 and provide the services you need.

If you are very advanced with computers, you might consider hosting your own web server but the average person needs to hire someone else to host their website files.

Your domain name means the website address

someone needs to enter to visit your website. For example, my professional website is www.sabrinasumsion.com. I did a search for that name and no one else was using it. Sometimes you have to do several searches on a variety of names to find one that is not already in use. Registering your domain name is typically very easy and most web hosting companies provide that service.

Hire an outside company
    If you do not have the time or desire to build a professional website, you can hire a company to build one for you. A simple web search for professional website provides tons of companies willing and able to build a site for you. The prices range from less than $100 to $1,000 and higher.
    If you choose to have an outside company build you a website, be ready with ideas on images, themes and content. These things will aid a person when trying to design a theme. In addition, have a budget ready. A lot of companies offer a la carte services so be aware of what you can afford.
    When deciding on which company to choose to assist you, ask for references. View other websites the company has designed. Make sure you like the over all attractiveness, flow and construction. If the sites look a little amateur, move on to another

company.

Personally, I have a favorite company to build websites but that is because it's my brother's company. You may be fortunate like I am to have a family member or friend that is able to build websites for you. You might tap into those resources first. If you don't have those resources, you can feel free to tap into my family resource. Just send me a message and I'll give you his Email address!

Blogs

The word Blog is short for "web log". It simply means an online log of events. Blogging is a popular activity across any country with Internet access. Simply put, you keep a journal online of your activities that anyone can read whenever they want from wherever they are.

Blogging as a publicity tool is useful to keep the information on your website updated regularly as well as create a place for fans to connect with you. I suggest that no matter what route you take to develop a website, a Blog is a must in the construction process.

It is very important though to write a Blog post regularly. Why is it important? It has to do with search engine rankings. Google, Yahoo, Altavista and other online search engines like to present their viewers with updated content. If you regularly post, their search engines will like you more and more and rank you higher and higher. This is important if you want new visitors to your website. (Which you do because that translates into potential sales.)

Social Networking

Also referred to as Web 2.0, social networking on the Internet is simply networking like you would do in business or plain life. The goal of social networking is to make connections or friends.

There are several sites dedicated to social networking such as facebook.com, myspace.com, twitter.com, linkedin.com and many, many more. You make friends, find past friends, post updates about your life and generally socialize. You can utilize those sites to make people aware of your book, its availability and events you will be attending.

The trick to effective Social Media, however, is to have a conversation with others. Social Media is different than sending out a newsletter or posting press releases. Social Media is about letting others guide the conversation as well as inserting relevant information to enhance your company or personal branding.

Produce, Publish, Publicize

There are some people who use their Social Media network only for posting ads. They talk about their product all the time and do not engage others about their lives. This is ineffective because people catch on quickly that you are not interested in them. When they figure out you are only interested in selling something, the6y will un-friend or un-follow you. Be genuinely interested in others.

Using the power of the web is an easy way to gain fan lists and create a connection to your best sales leads. For example, have a newsletter sign up on your website. The fact that a person is at your website automatically qualifies them as a sales lead. Try to get their contact information so you can contact them about sales promotions, upcoming events or ask for endorsements.

We live in an amazing time where you can connect with readers and fans that live across the earth in Australia or China. The Internet is an amazing publicity tool I recommend every person embrace.

Section 3: Publicity

Conclusion

Whew! The book is done! It was worth the effort to sit down, type it all out and then edit. And edit again. And edit again. Then send it to friends and family for their thoughts and fresh eyes. Then edit again. Then I sent it to the co-worker I mentioned who can catch most any typo and she found more errors. Then guess what I did? Yup. I edited *again*! Then I sent it to yet another person and he caught more errors! I sat down and edited again.

Yes, I'm tired of editing. Yes, I'm celebrating being done –finally! However, I am so proud of the clean manuscript and I feel the effort was worth it.

Thank you so much for coming on this ride with me. I am thrilled to have the opportunity to share some of the knowledge of the literary industry I have picked up over the years with you. I wish you all the luck in the world with your publishing ventures and encourage you to continue writing.

Book Group Study Guide

As you discuss *Produce, Publish, Publicize* in your book group, here are some ideas on questions to ask.

Do you have a book idea?

What is it?

Have you considered writing it?

Have you ever attended a class on writing?

Did you find it valuable?

What makes a good book?

Why would you write a book?

Which Publisher do you think would be best for you?

Would you try to find an agent or would you just try

to find any company to print your book?

When you buy a book, how do you usually find it?

Do you usually buy books online or in a bookstore?

Do you like meeting authors?

Have you ever attended a book signing?

Who was the author and why did you attend?

What do you think of book trailers?

What convinces you to buy a book?

Sabrina Sumsion is a publicist who has spent the last 5 years specifically working with authors. She has assisted authors with developing marketing plans, setting up online reviews, arranging newspaper articles, magazine features, radio interviews and television appearances. She has been referenced on several websites, she has been published in newspapers and magazines and has been on national television.

Sabrina runs her own radio show where she interviews experts from the literary industry. She is always searching for more information about the insider secrets in publishing for her listeners. You can listen to archived shows on Sabrina's website.

Sabrina Sumsion is available for speaking to groups. She is an experienced presenter who discusses topics ranging from publicity to autism. She runs workshops as well as presents as the key note speaker. To contact Sabrina about attending your next event, please call her at 402-484-8124 or Email her at sabrina@sabrinasumsion.com. To view more information about Sabrina, please visit www.sabrinasumsion.com.

Sanguine
Publishing

Sanguine Publishing is dedicated to releasing books
of value to the world. For more information on
titles available, please visit
www.SanguinePublishing.com.

LaVergne, TN USA
21 March 2010
176685LV00001B/2/P